Nicky Fifth's
New Jersey

by Lisa Funari Willever

Franklin Mason Press
Trenton, New Jersey

For Todd, Jessica, Patrick, and Timothy, the reasons I write.
And with love, for my dear friend, Sr. Marie Anthony

Special thanks to Anne Salvatore, Wanda Swanson, Dawn
Hiltner, and Iris Hutchinson, four amazing NJ women.

Franklin Mason Press ISBN 978-0-9760469-9-8
Library of Congress Control Number: 2011916998

Editorial Staff: Jennifer Wahner, Shoshana Hurwitz, Linda
Funari, Iris Hutchinson, and Mary Sullivan

Contents

The Nicky Fifth Series

written by
Award-winning author Lisa Funari Willever
Winner of the 2009 Benjamin Franklin Award

Book One
32 Dandelion Court

Book Two
Garden State Adventure

Book Three
For Hire

Book Four
Passport to the Garden State

Book Five
At the Jersey Shore

Book Six
Nicky Fifth's New Jersey

A Letter from the Author

Dear readers,

A funny thing happened on the way to book six. I invited children from all over New Jersey to submit their favorite Garden State destinations for Nicky Fifth and T-Bone. The responses were amazing, and by sharing their ideas and favorite places, my readers help Nicky and T-Bone bring New Jersey to life. When kids send suggestions to the soon-to-be Official Junior Ambassadors, they become ambassadors, too. Visit www.nickyfifth.com for great activities, tours, and upcoming contests.

As with **Passport to the Garden State** and **At The Jersey Shore**, you will find a passport in the back of this book, also. Read the story and ask your family and school to take you on some great N.J. day trips. You'll thank them *and they will thank you.* Always check the websites and call ahead to be sure hours and offerings have not changed. While we are always sad to see a Stamp Stop close, these are the risks of writing a book that blends fact and fiction. If a Stamp Stop is no longer operating, one of the other stops will gladly stamp that box for you.

Explore New Jersey, Enjoy New Jersey,
Lisa Funari Willever

$0.25 of each book sold is donated to Property of Pandullo for North/Central Jersey Walk Now for Autism Speaks.

Chapter One

It never failed. Every morning I ran downstairs to check the newspaper and every morning I was disappointed. Ironically, I wasn't even sure what I was looking for.

"Nicky," my mom sighed as she reached the bottom step. "I'm sure they'll call you or at least send a letter."

"What if we're wrong?" I replied. "What if I miss the article and never know that I am the Official Junior Ambassador of the State of New Jersey?"

"You mean one half of the Official Junior Ambassador team," said T-Bone as he entered the kitchen.

"Where did you come from?" I asked, really not knowing.

"I let him in," my mom laughed, "although I don't know where he went after that."

"Just tying a shoe," T-Bone explained as he polished an apple he found in our fruit bowl. We immediately looked at his feet and then looked at each other.

"Tommy," said my mom, "you say you were tying a shoe?"

"That's right, Mrs. A."

"And when you say tying a shoe, you're talking about actual laces, right?"

"Is there any other way?" he smiled.

"You tell us," I interrupted. "You're telling us you stopped to tie a shoe and *you're wearing flip flops*."

"True," he smiled, nodded, and took a bite of his apple.

"How did you tie laces on a flip flop?" I wondered. "How did you tie a flip flop with no laces?"

"I said I tied a shoe," he explained, "but I never said it was *my* shoe. I tied Maggie's shoe."

"Of course," my mom shook her head and smiled.

"Why couldn't you just give us all of the details at once?" I said. "You could've just told us what you were doing."

"Okay," he shrugged, "next time I tie Maggie's shoe, I promise I'll let you know. So what's going on?"

"Not much," I sighed as I paged through the newspaper once more. "There's still no word about our becoming New Jersey's Official Junior Ambassadors."

"Don't you think they would call us?"

"I guess," I agreed. "I just wish they would hurry up."

"Why don't we call Billy?" suggested T-Bone.

"No way," I insisted, "then we'll look too anxious."

"But we *are* anxious."

"I don't know. I think we should just wait," I said, even though I really wanted to call.

"What if we call Billy for another reason and see if that reminds him of anything?"

"That's not bad," I said. "What reason could we use?"

"Tell him we were curious if the state has any new roads, bridges, or ambassadors," said T-Bone.

"Are you serious?" I asked.

"Do you like how I very casually stuck ambassadors in at the end of the list?" he winked.

"Oh, yeah, that was *really* casual," I laughed.

"What's wrong with it?" he asked.

"We can't just ask about roads, bridges, and ambassadors. They don't even go together. He'll see right through us."

"Okay, Mr. Pending Ambassador," he squinted. "What amazing ideas do you have? Go on, dazzle me."

"How about we call Billy to see if he has any places he wants us to check out?" I suggested.

"That might work," he nodded, "but personally, I'd work roads, bridges, and ambassadors into the conversation."

Before he could finish his sentence, I had already dialed. Billy answered on the second ring, which was two rings too soon for me. My mind went totally blank. I knew I should have written down what I wanted to say. This wasn't the first time this had happened either. Every time I made a call, I would start to daydream after the first ring. My attention span would just disappear. The worst was listening to the automated choices. The robot voice would put me to sleep. By the time they finished telling me to press 1 for this, 8 for that, I'd need to press the star to repeat the whole menu. This call was no different.

"Governor's Office, Billy speaking."

"Hi, Billy," I hesitated. "It's Nicky and T-Bone."

"Hey, guys. How are you?"

"We're good," I mumbled while my mind scrambled to remember what I planned to say.

"That's great, just great. What can I do for you?"

9

"We were just wondering if New Jersey had any new roads, bridges, or ambassadors." I couldn't believe the words came out of my mouth.

"What's that?" he asked.

"Nothing," I mumbled. "I was just joking."

"Hey, that reminds me," he said. "I heard the Assembly Committee for Tourism and the Arts unanimously voted to move your bill to the General Assembly."

"That's great," I said. "I mean it sounds great. Is it?"

Billy laughed and explained that when a bill is written, it is assigned to a committee. In our case, the bill to name us Official Junior Ambassadors was written by two Assemblymen. It was then assigned to the Tourism and Arts Committee. They voted on it and it unanimously passed. Now, we were waiting for the head of the Assembly to schedule it for a vote with the whole Assembly. Then we would become Official Junior Ambassadors.

Wow, I thought, this is really happening. It seemed like yesterday when I was living on 5th Street in Philadelphia, hanging out with Joey Grapes and my Philly friends, living in a two-family house with my family and my grandparents. When I found out we were moving to New Jersey I thought I would hate the state. In fact, I planned on hating it. I even tried to talk my grandparents into renting me a room in their house. Then I met Tommy

Rizzo, *the famous T-Bone*. My parents invited him on our seven-New-Jersey-day-trip-substitute-for-a-Disney-vacation-extravaganza and that's where it all started.

The good thing was, when you're with T-Bone anything can happen, and it usually does. On our last Garden State Adventure that first summer, we ended up on New Jersey's radio station, NJ101.5, after T-Bone won their contest. The governor's office heard us talking about our day trips and invited us to be Unofficial Junior Ambassadors. Our job was to find, visit, and report on great places throughout the state. Apparently, people enjoyed our reports and now we were on the verge of becoming Official Junior Ambassadors. I still wasn't sure what the difference was, if there even was a difference. We did learn, however, that *official* and *unofficial* both meant not getting paid.

"Hey, I almost forgot to tell you something," said Billy. "I'll be sending over some fan mail."

"Really?" I asked. "For who?"

"For you guys," he laughed. "We invited kids to send suggestions of great New Jersey places you two should visit and we've received some amazing submissions. We even decided to name a winner to make it more exciting."

"How can you pick a winner when there are so many great places to visit?" I asked.

"That's exactly what we wondered. Then we decided to

select a winner based on how well they sold their idea."

"So they had to own the place, then sell it to New Jersey?"

"No, we judged them based on how well-written they were and which one would really persuade people to visit."

"So, you want us to judge them?" I asked, suddenly feeling very grown-up and very important.

"Actually," he explained, "we established a committee of librarians to follow strict scoring guidelines to ensure fairness. We'll be notifying the winner soon."

"If we're not judges, why are you sending them to us?"

"We thought they would give you more ideas and we wanted you to see how many kids have been following your adventures. Believe it or not, you have fans."

"That's amazing," I shook my head. "My mom will wanna frame each one."

"Your mom better own a frame shop," he laughed. "We've got quite a few letters here."

As we hung up, I started feeling pretty important, almost celebrity-like. Then my mom brought me right back to Earth by insisting I help my sister, Maggie, find her doll. So much for being a celebrity.

It took three days for the package to arrive and I can't say I didn't stalk the mailman. *I did.* I went to the front door every time I heard a truck, a car, or even a bicycle.

By the end of the week, there was a knock on the door. Please don't be T-Bone, I thought. Much to my relief, it was the mailman. It wasn't our usual mailman, Mr. Miller, but a substitute; a very uninterested substitute.

"Got a package for you," he said. "Sign here."

"You've got it," I gushed. "This is actually fan mail. From the governor's office in the State House. From our fans."

"Print your name here," he said, pointing to an *X*.

"Yeah, my best friend and I are about to be named Official Junior Ambassadors," I tried again to get a reaction. "It's pretty cool, you know."

"Have a good day," he said as he headed back to his truck.

Must not have heard me, I assured myself, as there was no other logical reason for him not to at least high-five me. I picked up this enormous box and almost tossed it over my shoulder. It clearly wasn't as heavy as it looked. In fact, it almost felt empty. I gave it a good shake to make sure it actually had something in it. Too impatient to continue the shake test, I carried the box inside and tore it open.

Chapter Two

The good news was that the box was filled with file folders that were filled with letters. T-Bone arrived within five minutes of its arrival and we each grabbed a folder. One by one, we started scanning the sheets. The letters weren't just ideas, they were also thank-you notes from kids for telling them about the great places in New Jersey. And they weren't just from kids, either; there were thank-you letters from parents, grandparents, teachers, and principals.

"Look at this," T-Bone pointed to a letter in his hand. "This one is from our old friend, George. He actually wrote a letter to the governor saying we are the best idea New Jersey has had in a long time."

"That was a nice compliment for us," I laughed, "*or an insult to New Jersey.*"

We settled in to start reading the submissions, but there were so many of them. After a while they started to blend together. I wondered how teachers were able to grade those essay tests they always gave. I decided if I became a teacher, I would only give multiple choice-tests. Scratch that. I would only give open-book, work-with-a-buddy, multiple-choice tests, with easy extra credit.

The more we read, the more we realized we had so much more to learn about New Jersey. Some of the suggestions we already knew about and some we had already visited, but there were so many we had never even heard of. I liked the idea of other kids becoming ambassadors by sharing their favorite places.

"We should separate all of the submissions into piles," I suggested. "We could have one pile for places we've been to, one for places we should check out, and one for the thank-you letters."

"That sounds good," he agreed, "but what about these?"

I turned my head to see him waving a pile of papers in the air. "What are they?"

"If I was a teacher, and not based on any type of personal experience, I'd say these are the kids that didn't read the directions. The folder says *Disqualified*."

"*Disqualified*?" I asked.

"What happened? The judges just didn't like their ideas?"

"No, that's not it," I laughed as I scanned the papers. "I'm guessing it's because this is a New Jersey contest and some of these suggestions are for Florida, Virginia, New Mexico, and Mexico. One kid even suggested we visit his house because he got new furniture."

"Wouldn't that be great if we showed up at his house and said we were there to check out the new couch?" said T-Bone, pretending to knock on a door.

"Could you imagine Billy's reaction if we gave him reports for Virginia and some kid's house?" I laughed. "I think we'd be fired on the spot."

"Can you really get fired from an unofficial job that doesn't even pay you?"

"I don't know," I shrugged. "Maybe ambassadors don't get fired. Maybe they make them leave the state."

"Well, if they kicked us out, I have some ideas of where we could go," he said with a big smile. "Florida, Virginia, New Mexico, and even Mexico."

The morning faded away and we were completely unaware of the time. We were so immersed in these submissions that we didn't realize we had missed lunch. That was shocking, since T-Bone's internal meal clock went off at exactly 12:00 noon and 5:00 p.m. daily. He must have been completely mesmerized by what he was reading.

We had them all sorted when I realized I hadn't seen the winner. Then I remembered Billy mentioned the winner hadn't been notified yet. We decided to call it a day. It was just as well. T-Bone and I had several odd jobs lined up for our company, *At Your Service*. Other kids thought we were joking when we told them we started our own business, but it was true. We had several customers around our neighborhood who hired us to do things that they either couldn't do or didn't have time to do. Since we started *At Your Service,* we had cleaned out garages, helped senior citizens pull out boxes of decorations, and even clipped their coupons. There was no job too big or too small and we accepted them all-- *except babysitting.*

The best part of our business was that it gave us our own money. Having learned about a little boy named Ryan Schultz who was fighting Duchenne muscular dystrophy and then little Joey Angiolino who died from Hurler's Syndrome, we decided to split our halves of the money four ways. Since I always kept my money in a sock in my sock drawer, it was a four-sock operation. We decided to save one-fourth of our money, spend one-fourth of our money, donate one-fourth to Ryan's Quest, the charity that is searching for a cure for Ryan and all of the other boys with his disease, and send the last fourth to the Duke Pediatric Bone Marrow and Transplant Program that helped Joey and his family. It wasn't like we were earning millions, but in two weeks, we had each earned $160.00. Not bad, I thought, considering we were kids.

In between our odd jobs, I continued to research great New Jersey places. I thought Billy's package of suggestions would make that work easier, but it actually became much more complicated. There were so many great ideas that we weren't sure which one we should visit first. It still amazed me that the fifth-smallest state had so many amazing places and things to do.

17

The next day, we stopped by our friend George's to pull weeds and thank him for the letter he had sent to the state.

"Well, it's about time we start recognizing good things when we see them," he said, rubbing his forehead. "You're promoting the state to young people, the exact people who need to know about Jersey so they can lead it one day. It's only common sense they work with you."

That was one of the best things about George; you always knew what he was thinking. He rarely held back what was on his mind and I liked that. I never had to guess if he was really happy with our work or with one of our ideas. If he said he was, he was. And if he wasn't, you didn't have to guess. I wished more people could be like George.

"Hey, George," said T-Bone. "Did you know Nicky is a *Great Debater*? Did he tell you about his trophy?"

Without turning his head, his eyes rolled in my direction. George had seen some of my finest speaking work when we first met him at the mall. He wasn't sure if T-Bone was joking so I smiled and nodded to confirm.

"Did you say *this* Nicky?" asked George.

"That's the one," T-Bone smiled.

"You mean the one who insists his tongue grows two sizes bigger when he has to speak to strangers or in front of a group of people? That Nicky?"

"That's the one," said T-Bone. "He came in second."

"Really?" he asked, raising one eyebrow. "Exactly how many participants were in this debate?"

"Just us," T-Bone proudly announced. "I came in first."

George smiled and shook his head as I rolled my eyes. That was the other great thing about him; it was like he could read my mind. With a simple eye roll, a smile, or a shrug, we could communicate. In that split second, George understood that I only did it for T-Bone.

"Please let me know when you have another debate scheduled," he grinned. "That's a show I'd love to see."

"You'd really wanna come and watch?" T-Bone asked in disbelief.

"I wouldn't miss it," he laughed. "But I do have another question for you. Where's your next day trip?"

"We were just talking about that this morning," I said. "Billy sent us some fan mail with lots of suggestions. We have so many ideas to choose from."

"This is New Jersey," he winked, "you can count on being busy for some time."

George was right. When T-Bone and I returned home, we decided to look over the suggestions again and figure out where we should go first. There was a great suggestion about a place called Grounds For Sculpture in Hamilton Township, Mercer County. It said there were amazing, huge sculptures and a restaurant called Rats.

"Hey, look," T-Bone gasped. "The chef was on the show *Top Chef.* That's un-be-liev-able. I love that show."

"Do you ever watch anything besides history shows and cooking shows?" I asked.

"Do they make other kinds of shows?"

"Okay, okay, I'll pull that one out," I said. "The idea came from a girl named *Brooke Bryant in Vineland.*"

"Should we send her a thank-you letter?"

"I don't know," I said as I scratched my head. "There are so many suggestions here. It might be a lot of work to send thank-you letters to everyone. Maybe Billy could put her name up on the state website."

"That's not a bad idea," T-Bone agreed.

It felt good to be putting another day trip together. Some kids might think the planning part was boring, but that was where the trip began. Finding all the places we would visit, getting the information, and making the itinerary was like a coach going over all the plays for the big game.

"Hey, Nick, listen to this," T-Bone interrupted. "The Howell Living History Farm is part of the Mercer County Parks, and they don't use any technology. They only use tools from 1890-1910 so visitors can see what life was like back then. A kid named *Robert Moran from Columbus* said you can make ice cream, build and race small wooden boats, help the farmers, and ride on wagons. That's definitely my kind of history."

"Great," I agreed. "We can give his name to Billy, too."

"Do you think we should check it out?" he suggested.

"Well, Robert seems pretty excited about it, so why not?"

Before I could finish writing some notes in our day trip notebook, I heard another gasp from T-Bone.

"Hey, here's an idea from a girl named *Melanie Gianinio in Wayne*," he said. "She suggested we go to a place called Allaire State Park because it's like, wait for it…traveling back in time. She said they have events that show you what life was like in the 19th century and tradesmen like a blacksmith, carpenter, and baker. You can see how kids' toys were made and how they baked in a brick oven."

"Very awesome," I agreed.

"She also said they have a school re-enactment, and it's right next to the Pine Creek Railroad where we can ride on a real steam train," he added.

"Got it," I said, trying to write as fast as he spoke. "Where's Allaire State Park, anyway?"

"New Jersey," he answered.

"I figured that. *Where* in New Jersey?"

"Looks like Farmingdale or Wall Township," he said.

"Oh, I remember seeing that on the map. It's real close to Belmar and Spring Lake."

"You mean it's at the shore and we missed it?" he shrieked.

"No, it's a little inland," I said as I ran my fingers across the road atlas, "but it's close to those shore towns. It's right off of Interstate 195."

I was excited to visit them all and really happy that we got these ideas from other Jersey kids. The Grounds For Sculpture sounded amazing and the restaurant, Rats, sure got T-Bone's attention. The Howell Living History Farm and Allaire State Park would be like the Old Barracks in Trenton and Historic Cold Spring Village in Cape May; great ways to actually see history in action.

It was hard to believe that there was a time when T-Bone and I really dreaded history. I realized we only became history buffs when we started seeing it and learning the stories behind it. Knowing dates was okay, but knowing about the people and the things they did on those dates was what got us really interested. Maybe if other kids saw the same things we saw, they'd be excited about history, too.

Just as I was about to suggest we call it a day, T-Bone jumped up from his chair and started waving a piece of paper in the air. His mouth was open and nothing was coming out of it. He repeatedly looked at me and then looked at the paper, still saying nothing.

"What's with you? Did we get a suggestion from George Washington's cook?"

"Even better," he exclaimed. "This is a suggestion from a girl named *Tessy Colegrove* who lives in *East Hanover*. She suggested we visit a bakery."

"A bakery?" I asked, hardly impressed. "Was it George Washington's favorite bakery?"

"No, it's not *just a bakery*," he exclaimed. "It's Carlo's City Hall Bake Shop in Hoboken. Ringing any bells yet?"

"Not really," I said, wondering why he was getting all worked up over a bakery. "Wait, does Hoboken's City Hall have a bakery in it? Now, *that* would be cool."

"No, think harder."

"Sorry," I shrugged, "I got nothing."

"You really need to watch more food shows," he said, still

waving the paper in the air. "This is the *Cake Boss* bakery. You know, Buddy the Cake Boss, Mama, *mia famiglia*!"

"Oh, right, I saw that show before," I remembered. "He makes these amazing cakes like a fire truck that has real lights and a building that has real smoke pouring out. But what does the *mia famibia* mean?"

"*Mia famiglia*," he said louder, as if that would make me understand another language. "It means *my family* in Italian. It's only the best food show ever created."

"That's great, but it's just a bakery," I said, then ducked.

"Just a bakery?" he asked. "Was Michelangleo just a painter? Was Michael Jordan just a basketball player? This isn't just a bakery, this is New Jersey history."

"Wow, how many seasons have they been on?"

"I'm not talking about the show," he argued. "I'm talking about the bakery. Did you know it's over 100 years old?"

"Keep talking," I said, suddenly interested.

"Yes, my bakery-challenged friend, according to Tessy, in over 100 years this bakery has had only two owners: Carlo, the original owner, and Buddy Valastro Sr. and family."

"Wow," I shook my head in amazement, "that Tessy sure did her homework on that one. She must be a huge fan."

"Read this," he said as he finally stopped waving the paper. *"Tessy is Buddy Valastro Sr.'s granddaughter. This is her family's business."*

I read Tessy's submission and it really was good. She didn't just tell us to go there, she gave us good reasons. Her grandfather first worked at the bakery and eventually bought it. When he died, her grandmother, her mom, her aunts, and her uncle took over. The bakery is still a family business and it was her second home. It was such a great story; it had history, family, New Jersey, and of course, T-Bone's favorite: desserts.

"Nick, we have to go there," he said, only two inches from my nose. "We have to go there. I watch the Cake Boss with my mom all the time. I know the whole family. There's Mama, she's Buddy Sr.'s wife; then there's the daughters, Grace and her baker husband, Joey; Maddalena and her baker husband, Mauro; Mary, and Lisa. Then there's Buddy, he's the youngest, and his wife is also named Lisa. Then there's the cousins and grandkids..."

"You realize that you don't really know them, right?"

"No, I do know them," he insisted. "I just haven't met them yet. We record every episode and my mom even tries to make cakes like Buddy makes for our birthdays."

"Really?" I asked. "How do they come out?"

"Not so good," he admitted.

"So, I guess you wanna go there?"

"Yes, I wanna go there," he exclaimed. "But we'll have to bring cold drinks and comfortable shoes."

"Why? Are we hiking to the bakery?"

"No, this place is a New Jersey landmark. Tessy wrote that they even changed the name of the street to Carlo's Bakery Way. People wait for hours to get in."

"Seriously, what do they do when they get in there?"

"They buy cakes, cannolis, éclairs, cupcakes, you name it. And if you're lucky, you can catch a glimpse of the family while they're working."

"Why are they still working?" I wondered. "Aren't they celebrities now? Why do they still work at the bakery?"

"Are you kidding me? This bakery is more than a lifetime of hard work. Television shows come and go, but this is their family business. They all still work there because they're the most hardworking family on and off television. Oh, my God, I have to tell my mom! She won't believe this!"

And with that, T-Bone did something he rarely ever did... he ran *out* of my house.

Chapter Three

It took a couple of days for T-Bone to recover from the excitement of Carlo's Bake Shop. We agreed that we would plan a day trip that included cold drinks, comfortable shoes, and a visit to see the Valastro family, even if it was a glimpse of one person over a busy counter. And that was if we were lucky.

In the meantime, we had to get down to business. I made a list of day trip ideas and decided to run it by T-Bone. As soon as he arrived, I knew something was different.

"Did you get your hair cut?" I asked.

"No," he stared at me.

"New shoes?"

"No."

"A new shirt?" I laughed, noticing his brand-new Cake Boss t-shirt.

"Yeah, my mom ordered it and it just arrived," he smiled and posed. "How's it look?"

"The shirt looks good," I noticed, "but I'd lose the pose."

"Very funny," he laughed as if I was joking. "So, what have you got?"

"I found some great places, so tell me what you think. We could do a trip to Hamilton Township in Mercer County and visit the Kuser Mansion, the Grounds For Sculpture, and Chick and Nello's Homestead Inn."

"What's the Kuser Mansion and the Chicken Yellow?"

"It's a restaurant, Chick and Nello's Homestead Inn, one of the Kuser family's mansions," I explained.

"Okay," he nodded. "So, who are the Kusers?"

"They were an important New Jersey family. They were rich, involved in politics and business, and they loaned the Fox Film company $200,000 to start the business. They had several mansions in New Jersey."

"Sounds like the Roebling family," noted T-Bone. "Did they make wire rope for bridges, too?"

"I don't think so, but I did find something interesting," I continued. "Do you remember our first day trip to High Point State Park and Lake Marcia?"

"How could I forget?" said T-Bone. "Your mom brought those Go-Away-Bear wands to scare away the bears."

"First of all, they were just red lollipops. Second of all, the Kuser family donated the 11,000 acres of land at High Point and the huge monument to the state."

"What? They owned the land *and* the monument?"

"Not only that," I began. "There's more."

"Okay, what else?"

"You might get mad when I tell you," I whispered.

"Why would I be mad?" he whispered back. "And why are we whispering?"

"Because they also donated a huge mansion that over-looked the mountains."

"So, why would I be mad about that? That's amazingly generous. Let's check out the mansion."

"Yeah, that's why you're gonna be mad," I whispered again. "It wasn't maintained and now it's gone."

"What? Why didn't someone preserve it? Don't tell me money. You can't put a price on history. Don't even tell me it was money. Whatever you do, don't say *money*."

"It *was* money," I whispered.

"Seriously?" he sank down in a chair.

"Yeah, but on the bright side, Annie from Cold Spring Village called us *Great Allies of History*, meaning there's plenty left to save."

"What else do we have?" he said, trying to recover.

"Well, another trip could be to that Howell Living History Farm, near Washington Crossing State Park," I suggested.

"That'll work.," he conceded. "What else?"

"There's one that will really grab your attention. And my father's, too, now that I think about it. Guess what it is."

"I give up," he said without guessing.

"All right, I shouldn't tell you since you're not even trying, but did you know New Jersey has a real rodeo? It's a real rodeo on the real rodeo circuit."

"Don't mess with me, Nick. This wouldn't be a good day for a practical joke, with the mansion and all."

"I know, I know, but I thought planning a visit to the Cowtown Rodeo might cheer you up."

"Nick, do you remember how excited I was when I found out about Wild West City? Do you remember, pardner?"

"Oh, no," I slumped over. "I forgot about your cowboy talk. You don't have to do that at a rodeo, do you?"

"Have to? No. Will I? Abso-rootin-tootin-lutely, pardner!"

And we're back, I thought. Good thing I saved the rodeo for after the Kuser mansion news. I was gonna tell him about Fort Mott, which was close to the rodeo, but decided to save it for another day. In fact, it was probably better to save the rest of my ideas for another day. This had been quite an emotional roller coaster for ol' T-Bone.

After he went home, I asked my parents if they knew about the Kuser family. My dad knew about the Kuser Park in Hamilton, but other than that, he couldn't remember anything about the family. I told them about the mansion and that I thought it was unfair such an amazing home fell into disrepair and no one did anything about it. My dad said it was the way of the world and since I couldn't change it, I shouldn't worry about it. My mom took another approach. When it came to things like right vs. wrong, good vs. evil, and underdog vs. favorite, she did not believe in rolling over. In these kinds of matters she was all about fight. There was nothing that annoyed her more than injustice, except for laziness and laundry on the floor. But injustice really annoyed her, much like it annoyed T-Bone. Unfortunately, I think I took after my father. I hated injustice. I hated decisions made for the wrong reasons, too. I just never felt like I could make a difference. Maybe that's the reason T-Bone and I made such a great team. I wasn't sure what I wanted to be when I grew up, but I hoped I would be someone who could make a difference when a difference was needed. I just needed T-Bone to rub off on me a little more.

Chapter Four

It didn't take long to plan a trip to Hamilton Township in Mercer County. There was more than one Hamilton in New Jersey and I never understood why people thought that would be a good idea. The Hamilton we were visiting was a large township in the center of the state. In fact, the exact center of NewJersey was in this township. My grandfather volunteered to be our tour guide since he had been to all of the places we would be visiting.

He arrived at 8:00 in the morning since Mercer County wasn't all that far from us. It was just a short trip up Interstate 295 North. T-Bone arrived right behind my grandfather and asked to check out the itinerary.

"What are you looking for?" I asked.

"Just seeing if Carlo's Bakery is on the itinerary."

"You know Hamilton is nowhere near Hoboken, right?"

"I know," he said. "Just checking."

It was weird seeing T-Bone without beach chairs, an umbrella, buckets, and a boogie board. Our last round of day trips included almost every beach town in the state and

T-Bone was like the equipment manager. Today, he only had the Flip Cam and some extra batteries.

"The Grounds For Sculpture first?" asked my grandfather.

"Sounds like a plan," I agreed.

"Do you boys know the history of the Grounds?"

"A little," I told him, "but I figured we'd learn most of it when we got there. Why? Do you know about it?"

"Now that you mention it, I do," he smiled. "Are you boys familiar with the company Johnson & Johnson?"

"Don't they make the yellow shampoo that doesn't make you cry?" wondered T-Bone.

"I know about that shampoo because I have little sisters," I said, raising my eyebrow. "But how do *you* know about it? You're the youngest kid in your family?"

"What?" he said as he started turning red.

"You use the little-kid shampoo, don't you?"

"No," he insisted. "I've seen the commercials."

"No, you use it," I laughed. "You use the same shampoo as Maggie and Emma!"

"It's not like I just started using it," he defended himself. "I kinda just never stopped."

"Don't be embarrassed," I teased. "Pretty soon, you'll be allowed to use big-boy shampoo all by yourself."

"Very funny," he said, turning toward my grandfather. "You were saying?"

"Anyway, the gentleman that founded the Grounds For Sculpture is J. Seward Johnson. His grandfather was one of the founders of Johnson & Johnson, the company that makes your no-crying shampoo."

"So that means he's rich?" asked T-Bone.

"They probably prefer wealthy," said my grandfather. "Now, J. Seward is a very talented artist and sculptor and he wanted sculpture to be a form of art that regular people could enjoy. So he bought the State Fairgrounds and founded the Grounds For Sculpture."

"So it's a little museum with some sculptures?" I asked.

"On the contrary," he explained. "It's mostly outside and people come from all over to see them."

I had a hard time imagining it, but the closer we got, the more sculptures we spotted. There were giant knights, a tooth, and a sailor and a nurse in what my grandfather called *The Famous Kiss*. T-Bone was confused.

"If all of the sculptures are on the road, why go in?"

"I'm sure there's more inside," I said.

"Oh, there's more," my grandfather assured us. "There's over 250 sculptures on 35 acres. I believe you'll be quite impressed."

My grandfather was right. It was huge and amazing, like walking into a different world. It was a combination park and indoor/outdoor art gallery. The landscaping was phenomenal and the sculptures were fascinating. It was better to see them outside instead of in a formal, white gallery. That's the reason Mr. Johnson created the Grounds. Interestingly, his work was my favorite. They looked like real people who lived in snow globes. T-Bone had a hard time selecting a favorite and I knew why. Every time we turned a corner, we found more outstanding art.

Until now, I always thought art was more for adults. Walking around the grounds, I realized how wrong I was. I couldn't imagine anyone, of any age, not being completely impressed with this place.

My grandfather decided we'd have lunch at *Rats* and it was a perfect day to eat outside. It was fancy and I asked if we should eat at the more casual *Peacock Café*. He told us next time we'd eat there, but today we were getting the full effect. As a top French restaurant, I was nervous to open their menu and hoping he didn't want me to eat a snail. Luckily, there was a delicious burger on the menu.

I couldn't wait to share this place with New Jersey. As we headed toward the exit, I thought I saw two kids running along the edge of the roof of a tall building. I grabbed my grandfather's arm and pointed, but nothing came out of my mouth. I was holding my breath, hoping they would move away from the edge.

"Relax," he smiled, "it's a sculpture of two kids running and I believe it's called *Following the Leader*. It got your grandmother pretty good on her first visit, too."

From the Grounds, we headed to the Kuser Mansion. It was situated inside Kuser Park, which T-Bone thought was convenient for them to build their home in a park that already had their name. When we explained that it was their country home long before it was a park, he didn't believe us.

"First," he began, "this isn't the country, it's a town. And second, they had a fountain and playground in their yard?"

My grandfather laughed as he explained that at one time, this was the country. Long before all of the houses and businesses this was the countryside compared to the bustling cities. Furthermore, when they sold the land and the mansion to the township, the plan was for the township to preserve it, turning it into a park and museum that everyone could enjoy.

"Just like that?" T-Bone asked. "They sold it?"

"Back then, many wealthy families, especially progressive ones, donated or sold land and homes to the state or towns as a way of preserving them," my grandfather explained. "As time went by, younger family members moved on, often unable to keep the expensive estates going."

"Like when Col. Kuser and his wife donated 11,000 acres, the monument, and the mansion at High Point?" I asked.

My grandfather turned his head in surprise. "You've done your homework, haven't you?"

"I also read that the Kuser family loaned Fox Films $200,000 to start what eventually became 20th Century Fox. I guess that was a lot of money back then, huh?"

"Still is," he smiled. "And when we take the tour of the mansion, you'll learn that they previewed the new movies right here in this house, before they reached the theaters. They even had a curved 18-foot screen, which at the time, was state-of-the-art."

As we approached the enormous house my grandfather told us that the estate was once 70 acres, but was now 22 acres. The home had 17 rooms including the dining room theater. There were many other buildings including a laundry house, coach house, barn, and garages.

"Hey, look," I said, as I pointed to the right. "Was that their tennis court?"

"Not only was it theirs," my grandfather noted, "that's one of the best clay tennis courts in the state. Many celebrities have played on it."

"Do you think the Cake Boss played on it?" T-Bone asked.

"Ignore him," I said, shaking my head.

As we walked in, I did what I always did. I imagined the people in the pictures living there. If I lived there, I would have climbed every tree on the property. I wondered if the Kuser kids climbed the trees. Without television and video games, I figured they probably did.

We learned that Rudolph and Rosalie Kuser came to the United States from Europe and settled in Newark. Years later, they purchased what would be known as the Kuser Farm, one of the finest around. A prominent family, they often hosted governors, senators, and celebrities. The Homestead Inn now sits on that land. They had six children: Fred, Anthony, John, Rudolph, Benedict, and Louise. Fred, often called Fritz, bought the land across the street from his parents' farm, now known as Kuser Park. He and his wife, Teresa built their summer home to enjoy when they weren't in New York City. Anthony Kuser owned the land, monument, and former mansion that were later donated for High Point State Park. The family was involved in many businesses, including the Trenton Street Railway Company, South Jersey Gas and Electric Lighting Company, the Hygeia Ice Company, the Trenton Brewing Company, and the Mercer Automobile

Company, which they brought to Trenton with the Roebling family. They were more than a wealthy family, though; they were very involved in the community.

"Wow," said T-Bone, "except for the wire rope, they really were like the Roebling family."

"You're right," my grandfather agreed, "the Kuser family had an enormous impact on the social, financial, and commercial growth of the city of Trenton. I knew a guy who grew up across the street from the mansion. When he was a boy, kids would sneak in and climb the trees and then climb across thick vines that connected the trees. They called the highest point *The Overlook*. Sometimes they would take grapes off of the vines or fruit from the trees and the caretakers would chase them out."

"You were friends with thieves?" asked T-Bone. "I wouldn't have guessed something like that. You always seemed so upstanding."

"No," my grandfather laughed. "I am upstanding and they didn't steal fruit to sell it; they would take an apple or pear here and there. Back then it was very thick woods that young boys couldn't help but explore."

"So you really knew people who knew them?" I asked.

"Sure," he smiled. "There's a gentleman named Tom Glover who keeps an amazing history of the township on a website for the Hamilton Township Public Library. He knew the family very well. If you visit his website, you'll read firsthand accounts from when he and his friend Don Slabicki worked for Fred and Teresa's son, Fritz and his wife, Edna. His brother, Bud, and Don's brother, Kenny, also worked at the farm."

"Are you serious?" asked T-Bone. "Do you think we could meet him someday?"

"I suppose we could stop by the library," said my grandfather. "Although I can't guarantee that he'll be there."

"That's okay," we said together, realizing this would be an amazing opportunity to speak to someone who knew the actual people we were learning about.

"Do you think he has some good stories?" I asked.

"His website is filled with them, as well as newspaper articles, many dating back over 100 years."

"I'd suggest that you read through his website and then we can stop by the library one day," said my grandfather.

As we walked through the house, each room was more impressive than the next. The dining room had heavy wooden chairs that looked like they came out of a castle. This was the room they also used as a theater room. The kitchen had a huge cast-iron stove, built-in cabinets, and high ceilings. For a house built in 1896, it was certainly in good shape. The house was filled with pictures and they were so interesting. There were black and white pictures of Lady Kuser on her horse and we learned that she was an avid equestrian. Then there was a wall by the steps filled with license plates and pictures of race cars driven by one of the younger Kusers. The bedrooms were neat as could be and it felt like someone would be returning home at any time. We heard that Lady Kuser still visits from time to time, or at least *her ghost still does.*

As we continued our tour, we were amazed at how large and modern the bathrooms were, at least for 1896. The playroom was filled with dolls and toys from that period. Fred and Teresa's room, like the rest of the house, had fancy wallpaper, heavy drapes and two beds, with a bassinet at the foot of one bed. This made sense, as they had ten children. There was also a fireplace in the corner. In the blue bedroom, the white and blue tiles around the fireplace must have been hand-painted and expensive because we couldn't find two that were the same. There were fireplaces everywhere and each one was unique. The dining room/theater was my favorite room and I could only imagine how exciting it must have been to watch new films, when films themselves were new.

"What did they do at the gazebo?" asked T-Bone.

"Oh, dear, that was built after Fritz and Edna, sold the house and land," our tour guides, Ruth and Ann explained.

"And the swings and sliding board, too?" he asked.

"That was also the township."

"How about that school at the end of the park. Did the Kuser kids go there?"

"Well," she said, "this was the Kusers' summer home, so they didn't attend school here and if they had, that school wasn't here. It was originally built by Monsignor Michael McCorristin from nearby St. Anthony's parish and was later called St. Anthony's High School. To honor his work, they changed the name to McCorristin Catholic High School. Several years ago, a number of Catholic schools in the area were consolidated and it became the Trenton Catholic Academy."

"Oh, I get it now," he nodded his head. "I thought it would be called the Kuser School."

"No," she smiled, "Kuser School is down the road."

"There really *is* a Kuser School? And a Kuser Road?"

"Yes, in honor of the Kuser family and their contributions. It's part of the Hamilton Township Public Schools."

"What a fascinating story," said my grandfather. "Thanks for your time."

I could tell my grandfather wanted to wrap it up before T-Bone thought of more questions. As we walked around the grounds, my grandfather told us that every December they create a Winter Wonderland with wagon rides, tree lighting, carolers, Santa, a petting zoo, and lots of food. He said the best part was the thousands of lights used to decorate the house, the trees, and the many buildings that lined that path.

"It must be really nice," I said.

"Your grandmother and I came once and it was snowing. It was one of the prettiest things I've ever seen. I think the Kuser family would have been pleased to see so many people enjoying their property."

"Do you think Lady Kuser shows up?" asked T-Bone.

"I don't know of any self-respecting ghost that would miss a party like that at their house," my grandfather smiled.

When we left the mansion we went right and followed the path along the park and behind Trenton Catholic. My grandfather told us that most years the boys' and girls' basketball teams were powerhouses in the state. At the end of the road we made a right and there was Chick and Nello's Homestead Inn, formerly Fred Kuser's parents' farm, right there on Kuser Road.

"Are we allowed in here?" I asked.

"Sure; it's an amazing, old-fashioned Italian restaurant," he replied. "You boys didn't even realize it was dinnertime, did you?"

Surprisingly, T-Bone's internal meal alarm never went off, although it was only a few minutes past five o'clock. The property really was right across the street from Fred's place. Pretty convenient, I thought.

"So this is where the Kusers first settled?" I asked.

"Not exactly," said my grandfather. "In 1818, Rudolph Kuser came to the United States from Zurich, Switzerland; first to New York, then Newark. He was a successful mechanical engineer and had purchased a home in Hackettstown. In 1867, he purchased this farm and moved here with his wife, Rosalie. He died here in 1891."

"When did Mrs. Kuser die?" T-Bone wondered.

"Well, Nicky, believe it or not, she lived another 32 years after Rudolph died, and was in good condition until the end. She was very close to her children and either saw them or spoke to them every day. She oversaw the homestead and Fred's farm and even though she never lived in Trenton, she had deep affection for the city."

"Sounds like a great lady," said T-Bone. "Did she ever eat here?"

"Here in her home? Yes," my grandfather replied. "Here at the restaurant? No, the restaurant opened after she passed away."

"Oh," he nodded.

When we walked inside, it was different than the chain restaurants we usually go to. The first thing we noticed was the delicious aroma coming from the kitchen. A man came up to us with a big smile and told us he would have a table for us in about ten minutes. There was a small bar area where we waited and I noticed three kids. T-Bone decided to introduce himself and found out that they were the man's children. It turned out that Danny, David, and Emily were actually triplets.

"Do you eat here often?" he asked them.

"Sure," said Emily, "my dad is one of the owners."

"That's pretty cool," said T-Bone. "Did you know that this place is very historic?"

"It was the Kuser family's homestead," said David.

"Yeah, this was their mansion," added Danny.

"We just toured the Kuser Mansion at the park," T-Bone informed them, "but they don't have a restaurant there. So what's your dad's name?"

"David," they all said together. "And that's our mom, Kathy, over there."

"Our great-grandfather, Nello, started the restaurant with his friend, Chick," explained Danny.

"His son, Jack, and his son-in-law Ernie also own it. And they each had sons, our Uncle Peter and our dad, David," Emily explained.

"So this really is a family business," said T-Bone. "Just like on Cake Boss."

"Is this your first time here?" asked David.

"Yeah," said T-Bone, "you have any recommendations?"

They all looked at each other and said, "The meatballs."

Before T-Bone could finish his game of twenty questions, David was bringing us to a table. We were seated next to a couple and their son, who was about my brother's age. As we walked past them, T-Bone studied their plates.

David came over and *told* us the menu. I was nervous because there was no star button to have him repeat it if I started to daydream. Luckily, everything he said sounded so good, I didn't miss one item. I ordered the pencil points and meatballs and my grandfather decided on salmon and green beans. We were waiting for T-Bone to make up his mind when he turned to the boy at the next table.

"Excuse me, my name is T-Bone and I noticed your dish when we walked by. Can you tell me what you ordered?"

"Sure," said the boy, "my name is Rubin and these are the veal tips. I think I order them every time we come here."

"So you've been here before?" T-Bone continued.

"It's my favorite restaurant," he said. "We come here all the time. Tonight, we're here for my tenth birthday."

"Hey, happy birthday, Rubin, how old are you?'

"Ten," he repeated. "Did you say your name was T-Bone?"

"It's actually my nickname. My real name is Tommy and that's my friend, Nicky, and his grandfather."

My grandfather and I both smiled and waved, while David patiently waited for T-Bone's order.

"You'll love this place," Rubin assured us. "The food and service are both outstanding."

"Any other recommendations before I order?"

"Well, the salad is really good and the tartufo for dessert is excellent. That's what I'm having."

T-Bone thanked Rubin and turned to Dave. "I'll take whatever he's having."

Rubin was right. The food was delicious and the service was so friendly. We noticed David knew a lot of the customers, but he treated us just as nice. My grandfather said that was the secret to a business that lasts and since they opened in 1939 it must have worked.

47

"How was your meal?" asked David. "Did Rubin and my kids steer you in the right direction?"

"Hated everything," we joked, even though our plates were so clean they looked brand new.

"David, did you know Rudolph Kuser?" asked T-Bone.

"Well," he laughed, "he was a little before my time. But you just ate in Rudolph and Rosalie's mansion."

"That's pretty cool," said T-Bone. "Do you know every person that comes in here?"

David smiled and said they have some people who come every week, but there are always plenty of new faces. His job was to make sure everyone felt at home, and we thought he did a great job of it. He even told us that there was a special table in the kitchen and the Switlik Parachute Company eats lunch at that table every day.

"Wow, when did they start doing that?" I asked.

"In 1939," David replied.

"When did they stop?" T-Bone followed up.

"Stop?" David laughed. "They still eat here every day."

"That's amazing," I nodded.

48

"Hey, I guess we're doing something right," he smiled as he walked back by the bar.

As we sat in the car and prepared to drive home, my mind was racing with all of the connections we had made. The Kusers were in the automobile business with the Roeblings, who we recently learned about. John Kuser owned a large estate in Bordentown where my mom took us for ice cream at *I Scream, You Scream*. Colonel Anthony Kuser donated the land and monument at High Point State Park, one of our favorite day trips. Suddenly that old, overused expression "small world" made sense.

Hamilton Township had made quite an impression on both of us. T-Bone told us he wanted to do important things when he grew up. I was going to tell him that we didn't come from the right kind of families: wealthy, connected, and influential. As I was about to tell him that it would probably never happen, I had a sudden change of heart.

"You're right, we should both do important things."

"Wow," he gasped, "I thought you'd say something like we shouldn't dream that big or we're not rich enough."

"*Who? Me?*" I laughed, wondering if reading minds was another one of his many hidden talents.

"No, I'm serious," he said. "I don't know what I'm going to do as an adult, but it'll be big and important. Maybe I'll end up really wealthy and donate things to the state."

49

"So, you're thinking you'd like to be a philanthropist?"

"I don't know about that," T-Bone hesitated. "I don't know if I'd like working in a drugstore all day."

"No," my grandfather laughed. "That's a pharmacist. A philanthropist is a wealthy person who donates to causes."

"Could I be a philanthropist that preserves historic sites?"

"Of course," said my grandfather. "You could save historic sites, preserve open spaces, and even donate to worthy causes, like the two charities you boys are saving money for now."

There was really no reason we couldn't be philanthropists. We just needed to become wealthy first. Being a kid, it was hard to imagine where to start, but I was sure all of the history we were learning would come in handy one day. Even though we didn't come from wealthy families, that was all right. I thought about Rudolph Kuser coming here at nineteen years old. I decided it was more important to be determined and hardworking than wealthy. In fact, not being wealthy would make us appreciate everything more. Plus, being wealthy didn't guarantee a person would do something meaningful, anyway. There were probably lots of lazy, rich people who never accomplished much. Some of them probably inherited their money and didn't know what it was like to struggle or save, and they probably never even *heard* of a coupon. I decided that determination was definitely more valuable than dollars.

Chapter Five

Two days after our trip to Hamilton Township, I was already preparing for our next adventure. Without telling T-Bone, I asked my dad if we could all go to the Cowtown Rodeo in Salem County.

"What?" he asked, pulling his head away from the newspaper. "There's a rodeo in New Jersey?"

"That's right," I laughed. "And before you ask, it's not new. Like Wild West City, it's over 50 years old."

"C'mon," he gestured toward my mom, "how do we not know about these places? I mean, a rodeo in New Jersey? When do you want to go?"

I was happy my dad was so excited. He had just gone through a rough period with his job and my parents had been on edge for a while. My very frugal dad just kept finding ways to save money. Since his job was secure, at least for now, I figured he wouldn't give me the do-you-know-how-much-one-gallon-of-gas-costs speech. And seeing how excited my dad and T-Bone were about our trip to Wild West City in Netcong, I knew this idea would be a slam dunk.

"I guess Tommy's coming?" he asked.

"Of course, dear," my mom smiled. "Both boys are going to be Official Junior Ambassadors. And T-Bone is like part of the family."

"Part of the family?" my dad exclaimed. "He's here more than I am! I almost listed him on my tax return. Last week, I brought home ice cream and realized I picked up *his* favorite flavor. *Again.* Don't they miss seeing him at the ol' Rizzo house?"

"Last time we were there his mom said that T-Bone was like concentrated laundry detergent..."

"A little goes a long way," my parents said together.

It was funny. As much as my dad loved to tease T-Bone and pretend he was at our house way too much, my mom and I knew the truth. He really did like him, which was good, because he really had become part of our family.

"So when can we go, Dad?"

"Go where?"

"Cowtown Rodeo!" I shouted.

"Oh," he shook his head, "whenever you want."

"Great! They run every Saturday from May until the middle of September. I'll call T-Bone and tell him we can go tomorrow."

"Great," my dad fake-smiled, "should we set a place for him at the dinner table?"

"Dad, now you're being ridiculous," I said. "Of course you should."

There was no time to waste, so I started printing information about the rodeo right away. Salem County was at the bottom of the state by the Delaware Memorial Bridge. Since the rodeo started at 7:30, I thought we could check out Fort Mott first.

I went on the N.J. Department of Environmental Protection website to look for some information about Fort Mott. They had some of my favorite things: a picture gallery, a virtual tour, and lots of details. I read the following:

It was part of a three-fort defense system designed for the Delaware River after the Civil War. The other two forts in the system were Fort Delaware on Pea Patch Island and Fort DuPont in Delaware City, Delaware. Construction was started in 1872; however, only two of the gun emplacements and two magazines in the mortar battery were completed by 1876 when all work stopped.

Fort Mott, along with Fort Delaware and Fort DuPont, became obsolete with the principal defensive installation on the Delaware River at Fort Saulsbury, near Milford, Delaware, shortly after World War I. Troops were regularly stationed at Fort Mott from 1897 to 1922. The federal government maintained a caretaking detachment at the fort from 1922 to 1943. New Jersey acquired the military reservation as a historic site and state park in 1947. The park was opened to the public on June 24, 1951.

Well, this trip should make T-Bone really happy, I thought. It was cool history and cowboys. When I called to tell him we'd be going the next day, I heard a big "Yee-haw" on the other end of the phone.

We decided to make a day out of it and do some exploring. The next morning, T-Bone arrived in jeans, cowboy boots, a plaid shirt, and a cowboy hat. Just as I was about to laugh, my dad walked out of the kitchen wearing almost the exact same outfit.

"You guys should really call each other before you get dressed," I laughed.

"Looking good, Tommy," my dad told T-Bone while ignoring my comment.

"Right back at ya, Mr. A.!"

"You guys look like you just stepped off a can of

baked beans," I said, laughing so hard I could barely talk. "Dad, you're not really wearing that, are you?"

"Why not?" he asked with a big grin, "I reckon this is what all the fellers wear at the rodeo. Wouldn't want to stand out, now, would I?"

"Dad, we're not going straight to the rodeo. You're gonna stick out the rest of the day. I'm telling Mom."

Before I could tell my mom, she entered the kitchen with Maggie and Emma in tow. Oh, no, I thought. They've all lost their minds. My mom's outfit almost matched my dad's, which almost matched T-Bone's. And my sisters looked like cowgirls from some kind of weird cowgirl beauty pageant. My only hope was that Timmy didn't go along with this crazy plan. Please let him look normal, I thought.

"Hey, I've got my cowboy stuff on," Timmy said as he walked into the kitchen. "How do I look?"

This was fantastic. We were about to be named New Jersey's Official Junior Ambassadors and T-Bone, my sisters, and my parents looked like they just finished a cattle drive, and then there was Timmy. My brother was wearing a Dallas Cowboys jersey and helmet and he had a football under his arm.

"I hope you all plan on saying trick or treat a lot," I said while shaking my head.

"C'mon, Nick," my mom hugged me, "get into the spirit."

"Yeah, pardner," T-Bone chimed in with his fake cowboy accent. "How's about you and I head down to the saloon and find us a sarsaparilla?"

"What?" I asked, more exasperated by the moment.

"I don't know," he shrugged his shoulders, "but it sounds cowboyish, right?"

"I'm getting in the van."

A moment later, the posse and the football player loaded into the van. We headed toward Interstate 295 and this time drove south. It seemed like the farther we drove, the more rural everything became. The southern counties were very open and green, with huge farms, long winding roads, and little traffic.

We got off of Interstate 295 at Exit 11 and started driving on Route 322. I was shocked that my dad opted to take country roads, but he said it would be dark when we left and this was the only way to catch a glimpse of *them there* farms. When we hit Paulsboro Road we headed south and then turned onto King's Highway. Soon, we came across a town on our left and my mom told us it was Swedesboro.

"They must have one great bakery," said T-Bone.

"Why?" we all asked at the same time.

"Sweets-boro," he answered. "It's named after cake."

"No, Tommy, it's Swedesboro," my mom explained. "One of the only two settlements in New Jersey established as part of the New Sweden Colony."

"Way to go, Mrs. A.! How'd you know that?"

"You boys aren't the only ones who can read about New Jersey," she said.

"Good point, but hey, stop the car, Mr. A.!" exclaimed T-Bone, forgetting to use his fake cowboy accent.

"What's wrong?" asked my dad, forgetting *his* accent.

"Look, on the left," T-Bone craned his neck and pointed, "there it is, just like I predicted!"

"There what is?" I asked.

"The Sweets-boro Pastry Shop! Do you believe it? I am a-ma-zing. Can we stop, Mr. A.? Please?" T-Bone begged. "I have my sock with my spending money."

"You mean you have your spending money from your sock, I hope," my dad said as he pulled into a parking space. "Please tell me you didn't bring a sock."

"No problem," he said with a great big goofy smile. "I won't tell you. I'll show you."

And with that, T-Bone pulled out a sock that looked like it swallowed Christmas. It was covered in reindeer, candy canes, and snowmen. Inside the sock was a wad of money. My dad just shook his head.

"Treats are on me," T-Bone exclaimed.

"No, Tommy," my mom insisted, "we're not letting you buy treats for everyone."

"It's okay, Mrs. A. My mom said to buy something for everyone, and I'm picking this."

"Yay, T-Bone!" my sisters chirped. "Yay, T-Bone!"

"Yeah, Mom," said Timmy, "if the man wants to buy treats, let him buy treats. We shouldn't be rude."

It was a small brick building and we could smell the deliciousness wafting to the street. The glass cases were filled with cakes, cheesecakes, pies, desserts, and breads. My dad even looked excited. We met the owner, Karen, and of course T-Bone told her about our pending ambassadorships. She was really friendly and it seemed like many of the customers were regulars. There were moms with strollers and some senior citizens and everyone just looked really happy. My parents ordered a danish, T-Bone and I ordered brownies, and Timmy and the girls ordered cupcakes. While my mom would have preferred to pay, she knew T-Bone really wanted to treat. As delicious as everything was, my dad's danish probably tasted even better since T-Bone was paying.

"Thanks, Tommy," my parents said at the same time.

"Yeah, thanks," added Timmy.

Emma and Maggie would have thanked him if their faces weren't covered with icing. It was in their noses and Maggie even had some on her forehead.

Our next stop was the Hancock House, and we drove right past Pilesgrove, where the Cowtown Rodeo was located, to get there. I decided to tell everyone about it. I had learned with my brother and sisters that if you just bring them to an historic place, they aren't very interested. When we told them all about it ahead of time, they were very excited.

"So," I began reading from the online brochure I printed, "the Hancock House sits on property that was purchased from John Fenwick in 1675 by William Hancock, an English shoemaker."

"Was he a cobbler like in my favorite storybook?" asked Maggie.

"Yeah, sure, he was a cobbler," I said.

"Did elves come in at night and finish the shoes because he was too tired?" she continued.

I was about to say no, but then I figured it might make my sisters more interested. I told them that every night elves did help him finish his work.

"Oh, Mommy, this is so exciting," she gushed.

"Upon his death," I continued, "the property passed to his wife and then to his nephew, John Hancock."

"No way," said Timmy, "the guy who signed his name really big on the Declaration of Independence?"

"No," I said, "I think it's a different John Hancock."

"Yeah, Timmy, pay pretention," said Maggie, "this man was a cobbler with elves."

"As I was saying," I tried to continue, "John's inheritance of approximately 500 acres made him a major landholder in Fenwick's Colony. He contributed to the development of the area by building a bridge across Alloways Creek in 1708. Now, known as Hancocks Bridge, it permitted passage on an important highway between Salem and Greenwich and gave the settlement its name."

"What were the elves' names?" Maggie asked.

"Ben and Jerry," I said, remembering the ice cream my mom brought home the other day.

Before I continued, I quickly read the brochure and decided not to tell the girls the rest. It seemed that this home was historically significant because of a British massacre during the Revolutionary War. During the winter of 1778, General Washington had sent one of his generals to South Jersey to forage for food, cattle, and horses. The British General Howe sent General Mahwood with 1,500 troops to do the same thing. The British met resistance from the Salem County Militia and local patriots. Frustrated, on March 20, 1778, General Mahwood issued the following order to his British troops: "Go-spare no one-put all to death-give no quarters." At approximately five o'clock in the morning of March 21, 1778, these orders were carried out. With local Tories who were loyal to the king and their slaves acting as guides, Major John Graves Simcoe and approximately 300 troops attacked the Hancock House where they knew the local militia was stationed. Of the ten killed and five wounded was Judge Hancock, who died several days later.

Since the girls were little, I didn't want to scare them and decided to just let them look for elves when they arrived. My parents, T-Bone and Timmy could just read about the history themselves. Before we went inside, Timmy noticed a strange pattern in the bricks on the side of the house. They were designed to make a pattern and at the top, in brick, were the initials WHS, which stood for William and Sarah Hancock, and the date, 1734.

As we toured the house, we learned Judge Hancock's great-granddaughter, Cornelia, taught at the Alloways Creek Meetinghouse School. During the American Civil War, she left for Gettysburg, where she served as a nurse. After the war, she directed the Freedmen's school for former slaves, founded the Children's Aid Society of Philadelphia, and helped plan Wrightsville, a model workers' community in Philadelphia.

"This house sure has an amazing story," I said.

"Yeah, there's just something about being in a real historic house," my mom agreed.

Everything was going really smooth until T-Bone walked up to the woman who worked there and asked if she had ever seen Ben and Jerry. The woman looked confused and started thinking, as if she should know them. When she said she wasn't sure, T-Bone asked her how anyone could forget if they had seen elves. Before she could respond, I grabbed him by the arm and dragged him into the next room.

"Did you seriously ask her if she ever saw the elves?"

"Of course I did," he answered. "Weren't you curious? I didn't even think elves were real."

"They're not real," I whispered. "I made that up to keep Maggie and Emma interested."

"So there aren't any elves?" he asked once more. "First, the Go-Away-Bear wands, and now this."

When I rolled my eyes, he told me he never really thought they were real and he was just joking. Sadly, I knew he wasn't. We finished our visit and decided to make our way to Fort Mott. It was only 11 miles away and the ride was very scenic. Fort Mott was located right on the Delaware River and there was a ferry that people could take to visit all three forts.

The website said that history lovers spend an exciting day in the 19th century when they take the round-trip boat excursions on the Delaware River. The Three Forts Ferry Service runs between Fort Mott in New Jersey, Fort Delaware State Park on Pea Patch Island and Fort DuPont in Delaware City, Delaware. From April through October, visitors experience authentic re-enactments of Civil War episodes, both civilian and military, "lantern tours" of the fort at night and demonstrations of how people lived in the 1800s. School groups are encouraged to visit this fascinating glimpse into the area's history. We decided that next time we came we would definitely take the ferry tour.

Hanging outside the fort was fun and while we were there we had about twenty relay races. While T-Bone could talk a blue streak, I could run one. Every time we raced, he came up with a different reason for why he lost. First, he claimed that he stepped on a rock; then he insisted he stepped on a turtle; next a bee flew too close to his ear; and then he was distracted by an ice cream truck. After beating him four times in a row, he finally declared me the winner.

There was a cool breeze and the sky was a perfect blue. Just when I was about to suggest we go get something to eat, my mom surprised everyone with a picnic lunch, complete with a basket and a blanket.

"When did we get the picnic basket?" I asked.

"It was a wedding gift. Your mom's been dying to use it since we got married."

"If I'd have known that, I would have suggested the fort a long time ago," I laughed.

"We weren't waiting for the fort to use it," he said. "We just never went on an *official* picnic yet."

"Way to be romantic, Mr. A."

My mom must have been really excited to use the basket, because she packed a feast. There were five kinds of sandwiches, strawberries, grapes, lemonade, crackers, and homemade cookies. Not only was it fantastic, it solved the mystery of what happened to the cookies I thought I smelled two days earlier. I had searched all over and couldn't find a crumb when I checked all of her usual hiding places. Clearly, she must have found a new place to hide cookies.

After lunch, we found some trails and took a walk along the river. It was a beginner's trail, so it was perfect for a family like ours with little kids and a worn-out T-Bone. It was such a nice day that we ended up staying at the fort for most of the afternoon. When we left, we drove by Finn's Point.

At Finn's Point, just outside Fort Mott Park, was a lighthouse. The tower was constructed in Buffalo, New York, and hauled by freight train and then mule-drawn wagons to its current location in 1876 at a cost of $1,200.00. At over 115 feet tall, the keepers would have to climb 130 steps and then climb a ladder, twice daily, to light and extinguish the flame. That's like extreme lighthouse caretaking, I thought.

On a normal day, we'd have probably been thinking about heading home at this point, but not today. Everyone was so excited that we got a second wind. While the rodeo started at 7:30, we definitely wanted to get there early and experience the entire event.

"Okay," I said as I opened my folder and pulled out some information I had printed, "this rodeo was started in 1929 by Howard Harris Sr. and his son, Stoney. It was an annual event until 1937, when World War II caused it to be put on hold."

"Wow," said Timmy, "1929 was a long time ago. They used horses then?"

"Of course they used horses," my mom laughed.

"Oh," he replied, "I thought this was a cow rodeo."

"A cow rodeo?" I asked.

"I don't know. It's called Cowtown, isn't it?"

"Yeah, that would be a lot of fun," I said. "Can you imagine a bunch of cowboys sitting on *cows*?"

"Sure, why not?" said Timmy.

"You've got to bring him to a farm," said T-Bone. "Even I know cows are too big to ride."

"Yeah, that's the problem," I said in my most sarcastic voice. "It has nothing at all to do with how little cows actually move. So, anyway, the rodeo outgrew the original arena and in 1967 Howard built the present arena with a seating capacity of 4,000. Howard Grant Harris, the fourth generation, grew up with Cowtown Rodeo. He was only one year old when the weekly rodeo started in 1955. He practically lived behind the chutes and at 8 years old, he won the Junior Bull Riding Championship. Grant entered professional competition at the age of 14, getting his Professional Rodeo Cowboys Association card at the age of 17. He entered Casper College, in Casper, Wyoming, with a full rodeo scholarship and competed hard all across the United States. In 1978, Grant, along with his new wife, Betsy, bought the Cowtown Rodeo from his father and had to make the very tough decision, to be a contestant or a producer."

"That's crazy," said T-Bone, "my mother would never let me ride a bull or a cow. So what did he decide?"

"Well, he knew it would be hard to run a rodeo and compete, so he gave up competing. His father and grandfather had spent their lives building the business and he wanted to continue the family tradition."

"That's a nice story," said T-Bone. "Kind of like how the Valastro family took over the family business."

"There's more," I continued. "Cowtown is not only unique because they've produced rodeos all over the East Coast, but they also raise most of their bucking stock. The bucking horses you see today are the grandsons and granddaughters of the bucking horses you might have seen in the early 1970s."

"Even the horses are part of the tradition," said T-Bone.

"I wanna be a rodeo cowboy," exclaimed Timmy.

"No problem, we'll start looking for a cow," my dad joked.

As we pulled in, everyone was dressed like my family. There were cowboy hats, jeans, and cowboy boots everywhere. I hated to admit it, but T-Bone was right. They all fit in. I was surprised at how big it was and with the parking lot filling up fast, we decided to find good seats first. I made sure I grabbed the Flip Cam, so I could get some video.

Once we got our seats, my dad, Timmy, and T-Bone went to get some food for everyone and I started filming. The air was still warm and humid as the band started playing country music. The opening ceremony was fantastic and involved a parade of horses and the national anthem. I checked out the program and couldn't wait for it to start.

The events included Bull Riding, Bareback Bronc Riding, Saddle Bronc Riding, Steer Wrestling, Tie-Down Roping, Team Roping, and Girls Barrel Racing. As the night went on, everyone in the stands became a cowboy. Everyone was cheering and clapping and the best part was that my dad and T-Bone forgot about using their accents.

"That was a-ma-zing," said T-Bone when the last event wrapped up. "Encore, encore!"

Suddenly, everyone near us turned in our direction. I knew they were all wondering if they heard him right.

"What are you doing?" I yelled to him.

"Encore means you want them to come out and do some more," he explained. "Encore! Encore!"

"Yeah, on Broadway," I replied. "Knock it off! People are looking at us."

"No good?" he asked.

I just shook my head. As we walked down the bleachers, I knew we were not going directly to the car. The girls wanted ice cream and my dad and T-Bone were itching to see some of the vendors. Forty-five minutes later, we headed to the van with half a dozen ice cream cones. Of course T-Bone and my dad each bought a big belt buckle and a new cowboy hat, while Timmy and I scored t-shirts. My mom bought Maggie and Emma those horse heads on a stick so they could pretend to be cowgirls. Maggie asked the man for a cow head on a stick for Timmy.

By the time we left it was pretty late and I was the only kid who stayed awake for the whole ride. Even though it was dark, I liked to see the names of the towns we were passing. We had already told Mrs. Rizzo that T-Bone would stay at our house, so we went straight home. My plan was to go home and start writing, but as Cowboy T-Bone would've said if he was awake, *I was just too tuckered out.*

Chapter Six

The next day was a Sunday and everyone slept in. When T-Bone and I finally made it to the kitchen, we saw my dad sitting at the table reading the newspaper.

"Good morning, Mr. A.," said T-Bone.

"Good morning," my dad replied. "Are you hungry?"

"Starved," I mumbled.

"Okay, great," he smiled. "Go get dressed."

"We have to get dressed for breakfast?" I asked.

"Don't be silly," my mom said as she walked in with my sisters. "We're going out. Here, grab a donut."

"Breakfast of champions," I sighed. "Where are we going?"

"We're not sure," my dad winked at my mom.

"O-kay," I said slowly. "You're not telling us?"

My dad leaned back from the table and placed his hands behind his head. "No, I don't think so."

"I'm in," said T-Bone.

"Of course you are," my dad closed his eyes and nodded.

T-Bone ran home to get ready and I ran upstairs to do the same. I had no idea where we were going and I was hoping I'd have a few minutes to start my report before we left. I sat down at the computer and started writing. Between the pastry shop, the Hancock House, Fort Mott, and the rodeo, there was a lot to share. I decided not to fix my mistakes as I wrote and instead wrote everything I could remember. At least this way I wouldn't lose any of my thoughts. An author who visited our school advised us to avoid editing as we wrote and fix our work later. I decided she had a point.

Just as I finished, T-Bone came walking in, wearing his Cake Boss t-shirt. At least this time he wasn't posing.

"So where are we going?" he asked.

"I don't know," I answered.

"Did we plan another day trip that I don't know about?"

"Don't look at me," I shrugged.

We went downstairs and asked my dad where we were going, *again*. He told us we would see when we got there. A strange feeling washed over me. I was usually the one planning where we went and in what order. This definitely

71

felt strange. My mom said we should take one day and just enjoy the ride. The thought hadn't crossed my mind. Lately, everything I thought about had something to do with New Jersey and day trips. I ran in to get my notebook and the Flip Cam, just in case.

After a bunch of back roads, we headed east on Interstate 195. I knew this was the way to the shore, but we didn't have bathing suits, towels, chairs, and the 99 other things we drag to the beach. We got off at Exit 11 for Allentown, turned onto Stone Tavern Road, and arrived at the Horse Park of New Jersey.

"I wish I would have known we were going to a horse farm," said T-Bone. "I left my cowboy hat at home."

"Darn," I said as I snapped my finger. "Now what'll you do, pardner?"

"Very funny," he laughed.

"What is this place?" asked Timmy. "Is it another rodeo?"

"No," said my dad, "it's a place where they have horse competitions and agricultural events. I'm not sure if anything's going on today, but I thought we'd check."

Something must have been going on, I thought, as there were so many cars in the parking lot. It turned out that it was a 4-H show.

"Look," my mom said to Maggie and Emma, "they'll have animals here."

"I wanna see dinosaurs," said Maggie.

"No, honey," said my mom, "dinosaurs are at museums."

"Then I wanna see a scary lion," she declared. "And I wanna feed him popcorn."

"Sorry, honey, lions live at the zoo and you shouldn't feed them popcorn, anyway."

"Then can I see a cobbler's elf?" she pleaded.

I knew that story about elves at the Hancock House would come back to haunt me.

"Let me," said T-Bone as he bent down to Maggie's level. "This is a 4-H animal show, so we'll see horses, hippos, hyenas, and hamsters."

"What are you talking about?" asked my dad.

"It's a 4-H show," T-Bone explained his logic. "It's about animals that start with H."

"No, it's not," my dad corrected him. "Where do you come up with these things? It's an agriculture show with animals, fruits, and vegetables."

"Even animals that don't start with *H*?"

"I believe 4-H is about hands-on learning," my mom interrupted. "There are four H's in 4-H. They're the four values members work on through fun and engaging programs: Head, Heart, Hands and Health. It's a great organization for kids in all communities, not just rural."

"How'd you know that?" I asked.

"We really knew we were coming here, so I did my own research," she smiled. "And for you history buffs, 4-H has been around for over 100 years."

"So what do they do?" I asked. "Is it just farming stuff?"

"I thought it was until I read a little more. Each club focuses on topics of the members' choice. They conduct project-related activities. A gardening club may have a year-round garden or a technology club may work on Web design at meetings. 4-H clubs also do community service both in their project area and where they are needed."

"That's awesome," said T-Bone. "I mean hippos would have been cool, but this is really good. I wonder if they have debate projects."

"Hey, look over there," I pointed to some goats, desperately trying to distract him.

We ended up staying for a couple of hours and made sure

we grabbed a brochure before we left. They held horse jumping shows and even had a hoedown. I wasn't sure what a hoedown was, but it sounded like a good time. I had a feeling we'd be back, especially since my dad and T-Bone had new belt buckles and cowboy hats.

I wasn't sure if we were going home, but when my dad continued on Interstate 195 east, I knew we weren't done. I was starting to enjoy being a plain old passenger and not the trip coordinator. Soon we were almost at the end of the road, which was confusing. I had no idea where we were going, but I also knew the ocean was straight ahead and we'd be running out of land soon.

We took Exit 31A for Allaire State Park. T-Bone and I both looked at each other and said, "Melanie Gianino."

"What?" asked my mom.

"Melanie," I said. "A girl named Melanie suggested we come here. She said it was awesome."

"It looked awesome on the internet," she smiled.

"You researched this, too?" I asked.

"I guess you're rubbing off on me," she laughed.

Besides being an enormous park that even had camping, there was an historic village, a train, and a full calendar of events. By the time we arrived, we were starving. My mom noticed a food vendor and quickly grabbed some hamburgers, hot dogs, and lemonades. We weren't sure what to do first, and then we saw the Visitors Center. There were exhibits on the 19th-century bog iron industry and the Howell Works, the original name of Allaire Village.

I read that in 1822, James P. Allaire bought the village that now bears his name and the 5,000 acres in the vicinity for $19,000, establishing the Howell Works. It was a major center for the production of bog iron.

"Hey, listen to this," T-Bone started to read. "Between 1827 and 1837, Mr. Allaire replaced many of the wooden buildings and the mill that was there before he bought it. He built large brick buildings and then created a self-sufficient village for his workers."

"That's right," said my mom. "There were 25 buildings and about 300 people who lived here. There was a carpenter shop, blacksmith shop, gristmill, bakery, school, church, post office, and apothecary."

"A-poth-a-what?" asked T-Bone.

"Oh, sorry," my mom laughed, "it's like a drugstore."

"This reminds me of the town of Roebling," I noticed, "creating a whole community for the workers."

"That's an astute observation," my mom teased. "Did you also know that, of the twenty-five original buildings, thirteen still exist? There's a chapel where his daughter was married and where couples are still married today."

"So what did they make at an iron bog?" asked T-Bone.

"For quite some time, the New Jersey Pine Barrens were filled with bog iron blast furnaces," my dad explained. "The furnaces used bog iron, a renewable resource found on the flood plains and swamps, to make iron. The blast furnace used bog iron and things like oyster shells and charcoal to make iron products."

"Sounds hard," said T-Bone. "It might have been easier for them to buy those things at the General Store."

"Tommy," my dad sighed, "where do you think the General Store got the iron items?"

"Good point, but why aren't they making iron right now?"

"Developments made it impossible for bog iron to compete with cheaper products that were just as good."

"So who lives here now?" I asked.

"No one lives here," my mom explained. "Mr. Allaire lived here with his second wife and his son, Hal, until his death. The Allaires were great supporters of free education, even for girls. After Mrs. Allaire died, Hal lived here, mostly alone, while it fell apart around him. People even called it the Deserted Village. "

"Why didn't he fix it?" I asked.

"Probably too expensive without the iron making."

"I guess," T-Bone agreed with my dad.

"You know there was another person who played a large role in this becoming a state park," said my mom.

"Was it a Kuser?" I asked.

"Was it a Roebling?" shouted T-Bone.

"No," she laughed. "It was man who doesn't get much credit. His name was Arthur Brisbane and he was the highest-paid journalist/editor in the world. He even interviewed President Hoover. He bought it in 1907 and eventually built a mansion where he and his wife first used it as a summer home; then as their permanent home."

"This place has some history," I remarked. "Did Mr. Brisbane give it to the state?"

"At the time of his death, he was in the process of giving the land and the village to the state so they could create a park," she said. "He ensured it would be preserved."

"See, that's what I want to do," said T-Bone, "but *before* I die."

"Good idea," I said, realizing that we had only scratched

the surface of the Allaire State Park history. We left the Visitors Center to check out the buildings. We came across the row houses and were even able to go in one. We stopped by the Blacksmith Shop, the Tinsmith Shop, the Carpenter Shop, and even the mansion. Costumed interpreters were giving demonstrations and it reminded me of Cold Spring Village in Cape May. Of course, there were two shops we wouldn't miss: the bakery and the General Store.

We grabbed some treats and more cold drinks at the bakery and then my mom led us to the General Store. It was huge and they sold everything from candy to toys and souvenirs to decorative items for the house. My mom bought some kind of a candle holder when my dad wasn't paying attention and the rest of us picked out some candy. Before we left we checked out the train. It was just getting ready to leave, so my dad suggested we go for a ride.

"I love this place," said T-Bone as the train pulled away.

"Me, too," Emma clapped as she sat on my mom's lap.

The train returned about half an hour later and we headed to the van. Good thing I brought my notebook and camera, I thought. This turned into an *unofficial official day trip!*

Much to my surprise, my dad headed north instead of west to go home. As we entered the Garden State Parkway, T-Bone told us this was his favorite highway in the state. *Turns out he just liked the name.*

"Where we goin'?" I asked. "This isn't the way home."

"You're right," said my dad, keeping it a surprise again.

Before I knew it we were at Pier Village in Long Branch and I was hoping they were taking us to Stewart's Root Beer. It was dinnertime and I personally thought that would have been a great place to eat. A breeze was coming in off the ocean and it was noticeably cooler here. My dad headed straight to Stewart's.

It was such a beautiful day so we decided to eat outside. T-Bone immediately introduced himself to a hostess who had no idea who he was. She stared at him for a moment and said, "Okay, nice to meet you."

Since there were seven of us, my parents and sisters sat at one table and T-Bone, Timmy, and I sat at a table on the other side. My mom seemed uncomfortable having us so far away, but my dad said, "What could go wrong?" We almost felt like adults.

As we looked over the menu, I had trouble deciding what to order. I found that I usually had two restaurant problems: those with nothing I liked on the menu and those with everything I liked on the menu. T-Bone must have felt the same way, because he pulled the same move that he pulled at the Homestead Inn. He leaned over to the woman and kids at the next table and asked what they were having and what they recommended.

"Everything's good here," the woman smiled. "We're having pork roll and cheese."

A Jersey delicacy, I thought. That might be the way to go.

"Hi, I'm T-Bone and this is my friend, Nicky and his brother, Timmy," he smiled. "Nicky and I are about to be named New Jersey's Official Junior Ambassadors."

"What's he doing?" Timmy whispered as we both smiled and waved.

"Congratulations! I'm Lisa and these are my kids, Teresa and John, and this is their cousin, Lucia. So what do Official Junior Ambassadors do, anyway?"

She was very friendly, even though she seemed a little confused. I gave her credit for not getting up and moving.

"We find, visit, and report on great New Jersey places and the state puts our reports on a website."

"That's very nice," she smiled. "Good for you."

"We already put this place in one of our reports when we came here last time," he continued. "Did you know they have statues of presidents that stayed here down on the boardwalk?"

"I did know that," she answered.

"Did you know they have a great bakery called Cake, Bake, and Roll?"

"We go there all the time. We like cake," said John as he smiled at his mom.

"You may think you like cake, but I love cake," said T-Bone, standing up and modeling his Cake Boss t-shirt.

Oh, no, not the pose, I thought.

"That's very nice," she said. "Have you ever been there?"

"No," he shook his head as he sat back down. "But we're gonna write a report about it. We're going up there and bringing comfortable shoes and water bottles.

"Are you hiking there?" she asked.

"No, I watch the show," he replied. "There's always a long line and I want to be prepared."

As T-Bone and Lisa were speaking, Timmy and I noticed all of the kids giggling and whispering. At first I thought it was just the goofy pose, but then I realized something else was going on.

Teresa stood up and she was wearing the same exact shirt as T-Bone.

"No way," he said. "Have you ever been there? How long

did you stand in line? Did you get a cannoli? Did you see Buddy or his sisters or no, hold on, did you see Mama?"

"Yes, I've been there," she giggled, "and no, I didn't wait in line, I have had the cannoli, and I've seen Buddy, his sisters, and Mama."

"Wow, you hit the Cake Boss jackpot!" T-Bone gushed. "Are they as nice in person as they are on television?"

"Nicer," said Lucia.

"You met them, too?" he gasped.

At this point, the waiter who was about to take our drink order must have decided to come back later. Before I could stop him, he had walked away.

"Tell him, Mom," John said as he nudged Lisa.

"You, too?" he gasped. "Did you win some kind of a contest? I am dying to meet them. I know them all: Buddy, Lisa, Maddalena, Mauro, Mary, Lisa, Grace, Joey, Anthony, and Mama. Even cousin Frankie."

"Really?" asked Lisa with a big smile. "You know them?"

"Do I know them? Are you kidding? Do I know the Valastros? Like they're my own family," T-Bone gushed.

"Would you know them if you saw them in person?"

"From a mile away."

"Even if one of the sisters was sitting at Stewart's, in Long Branch, wearing sunglasses?" she said as she slid her glasses to the top of her head.

"Oh, my God!" T-Bone shrieked. "You're Li-Li-Lisa and oh, my God! No way! No way! You're Lisa. Teresa, your mom is Lisa."

"Hi, T-Bone, my name is Lisa Valastro," she smiled.

"Nick, Nick," he grabbed my arm, "do you know who this is? Do you have any idea who this is? I'm serious. Guess who this is?"

"Lisa Valastro," I said, and waved to her. Leave it to T-Bone's dumb luck to plant us right next to his baked goods heroes. If my parents picked our table instead of us, we would have never even realized who they were.

"So you're a fan of the show?" she laughed.

"He's the kind of fan you need security for," said Timmy. Suddenly, Teresa was whispering in her mom's ear. Lisa turned and looked at us and then spoke to Teresa again. I hoped they weren't about to call the police.

"Boys, you said you're about to be Official Junior Ambassadors?" she asked.

84

"Yes, ma'am," said T-Bone. "Me and my, uh, friend here, uh, that one."

Wow, he forgot my name and called her ma'am. I figured T-Bone's tongue must have swelled up. Mr. Smooth-talker was tripping all over his words. He really was starstruck.

"Well, Teresa heard about a New Jersey contest at school and she wrote about the bakery and its history. Was that *your* contest?"

"Yes! Well, it's actually the state's contest, but it's for kids to tell us their favorite places so we can visit them and write reports about them," I answered, knowing T-Bone would never be able to get it out.

"Boys, we got a letter from the state yesterday," said Lisa, almost as excited as T-Bone. "Teresa won your contest. She's a very good writer and her teachers suggested she enter! Oh, my God! This is so exciting! Oh, my God!"

It was hysterical that now Lisa was as excited about the contest as T-Bone was about meeting her. I thought it was pretty cool that even though she was a celebrity, she was really excited about the contest. Her excitement was contagious and everyone started high-fiving each other; everyone except T-Bone.

"Wait a minute," he said in a very serious tone. "We actually got a few submissions for the bakery, but I don't remember one from a Teresa."

"Was there one from a Tessy?" asked Teresa with a grin.

"Yeah, and I hate to say this and ruin the excitement, but the submission from Tessy was awesome," he said, not making the connection. "This might be an awful mistake because I don't remember anything at all from a Teresa."

"You're not getting it," said John, as Lucia and Teresa giggled. "Teresa's nickname is Tessy."

"What?"

"My sister's name is Teresa, but we call her Tessy!"

"No way!" said T-Bone as he jumped back up again and hugged Lisa. "No way, this is amazing! I don't, I don't, I don't even know what to say. You've won! You're the winner! I don't even know what you've won, but you've won! Wow, I hope it's a cruise or a car."

I thought it was a small world a couple of days ago. Now, I could have fit the world in my pocket. Our excitement spread throughout the restaurant and soon everyone was cheering and clapping. "Congratulations!" T-Bone announced for everyone outside to hear, "Tessy is the winner of the New Jersey contest! Tessy is the winner!"

Suddenly everyone who was eating outside and people who were walking by started clapping and whistling. My mom jumped up and ran to our table, totally regretting the decision to let us sit so far away.

"Tommy, Tommy," she whisper-yelled. "What are you doing? Shhh! Why are you yelling? Stop doing that!"

When T-Bone explained everything, my mom looked more confused. When Lisa explained everything, my mom understood. Eventually we ordered and my family moved to a table next to us that had just opened up. Wow, I thought, T-Bone couldn't have dreamed a more perfect day. They were all so nice and excited about Tessy winning the contest. It was awesome. My mom and Lisa hit it off immediately and I heard them talking about Carter and Cavero, the Old World Olive Oil shop. The rest of us spent the whole meal talking to Tessy, John, and Lucia. Tessy was ten years old, John was eight, and Lucia was seven. I couldn't believe how nice they were. T-Bone still couldn't believe they didn't have to wait in line.

"Well, you can leave the comfortable shoes and water bottles home," said Lisa. "When you come up as our guests, you won't need to stand in line."

"Wh-at? Are you kidding me?" T-Bone exclaimed. "Oh, my God, this just keeps getting better. You know you're the best show for showing a real New Jersey family."

Before she left, she signed T-Bone's shirt, even though he wanted her to sign his forehead. She gave her contact information to my mom and invited all of us to come and tour the bakery and meet everyone.

"I'm sorry, did you say tour the bakery and did you also

say meet everyone?" T-Bone whispered.

"Well, if you want to write a report about the bakery, you need to see it and meet everyone, right?" said Lisa.

"When you say everyone, does that also mean Mama?"

"Absolutely," she laughed. "She's retired now, but when I tell her about you, she'll definitely come in."

"You're going to tell her about me?" he asked.

"I'm going to call her and tell her about you as soon as we get back to the house!" said Tessy.

When we left Stewart's, we headed over to Carter and Cavero Old World Oils. I assumed that was the real reason we had ended up in Pier Village. They had barrels of oil with little spouts and cubes of crusty Italian bread to sample the oils. Even though I was kind of full, I figured I should try some. Lisa's recommendation was so good, my dad, *without a single coupon*, bought three different bottles.

As we headed to the van, T-Bone had a smile plastered on his face. In all the time I had known him, I had never seen him become so unglued. I was kicking myself for not filming it. Not only was this an amazing opportunity to meet the Valastro family, we would have definitely won the grand prize on the funny video show.

Chapter Seven

After two back-to-back day trips, even though one was unplanned, we were exhausted and exhilarated. Instead of being too tired to think about our next day trip, I was more energized than ever. In fact, I was so excited I wanted to go everywhere. I shuffled through the submissions Billy had sent us and remembered the one from *Robert Moran* at *Mansfield Township Elementary School*. He suggested we visit the Howell Living History Farm in Mercer County. When I went on their website, I knew it would be interesting, I just didn't realize the world would get even smaller.

When I searched for information on the farm, I learned many interesting things, including an amazing connection. Mrs. Inez Howe Howell, the widow of Charles Howell, donated the 128-acre Howell Farm to the Mercer County Parks Commission to be used as a Living History farm. Her intent was for people, especially children, to see how a farm worked and appreciate its contributions to everyone's lives. It was a generous donation and reminded me of the Kuser family. As I continued to read, I learned that Inez Howe Howell and Edna Howe Kuser weren't just generous women, *they were sisters*.

I called T-Bone to share what I had stumbled upon, but it took ten minutes for him to get past a woman named Howe marrying a man named Howell.

"Seriously?" he asked. "Inez Howe married Charles Howell? Too funny."

"No, that's not the ironic part," I insisted. "Inez Howell and Edna Kuser were actually sisters."

"That's cool, too," he agreed. "But I think the name thing is a little funnier."

"Whatever," I said. "So what do you think?"

"Do they have a bakery?" he asked.

"I don't know. Maybe. Does it matter?"

"I guess not," he said. "I should probably stop eating baked goods for a while, anyway."

"Why?" I asked.

"Because I'm bringing my sock to Carlo's Bake Shop and I'm eating my way from one end of the case to the other," he laughed.

"Great," I said, "but what about visiting the Howell Farm? Are you in?"

"I'm always in," he replied. "Are you also checking out Washington Crossing State Park?"

"I'm on it," I said. "Do you want to come over now and work on the plans?"

I waited for him to answer and asked again. I wasn't sure if he had another call and I missed him telling me to hold on, so I waited. "Hello? Hello? Are you still there?"

"I'm right here," he said, standing in my doorway, out of breath and panting.

"What are you trying to do, break the land speed record?" I joked, still amazed at how fast he could be at my house.

"You know, it would have been easier if your parents bought the house next door to me. Then I could get here even quicker."

"Yeah, that would have been a real selling point for my dad," I told him.

"What have we got so far?" he asked, grabbing the atlas.

"Well, we have the Howell Farm and Washington Crossing State Park, so far. I'll keep looking."

About ten minutes later, I was on to something. I was reading about the Delaware & Raritan Canal. It was actually a state park and part of it ran between the

Delaware River and Route 29 from Trenton to Frenchtown. Since both the farm and the park were off of that road, it would be a good idea to check it out.

"Hey, T-Bone," I said, "we could go to Washington Crossing Park, then cross the street to the Delaware-Raritan Canal State Park and then up the road to the Howell Farm."

"Is it like the Panama Canal?" he asked.

"How would I know?" I replied. "I don't know anything about the Panama Canal."

"You don't?" he asked, as if everyone knew about it.

"No, do you?"

"No, but they're both canals," he grinned.

"Anyway," I continued, "the history is pretty interesting."

"One question," he stopped me, "what exactly is a canal? I never really knew the difference between river, lake, pond, stream, creek, and canal."

"Actually, I just looked it up myself," I admitted. "I wasn't sure either. It says it's an artificial waterway."

"So, it's fake?" he asked.

"I think they mean man-made."

"Man-made?" he gasped. "How could people make a canal? Have you ever seen how long it takes to dig a hole for one in-ground pool?"

"No, have you?"

"No, but I'm sure it takes a while," he said. "If it runs along the river, why didn't they just use the river?"

"Their website says that during the early nineteenth century, when the United States entered into the Industrial Revolution, canals were built as transportation routes to link resources, manufacturing centers, and markets. The D&R Canal was built across central New Jersey to provide an efficient and safe route for transporting freight between Philadelphia and New York," I read. "Maybe the river would be too rough or didn't go exactly where they needed it to go."

"How long is it?" he asked. "A few miles?"

"It says construction began in 1830. The main canal was 44 miles long, 75 feet wide, and 7 feet deep. The feeder was 22 miles long, 50 feet wide, and 6 feet deep."

"Wow, they must have needed at least 500 bulldozers."

"Yeah, funny thing," I told him, "laborers, most of them Irish immigrants, were hired to dig the main canal and its feeder. It says they dug mostly by hand. It doesn't say anything about bulldozers."

"Dig? By hand? Just people and shovels?"

"That's what it says," I shrugged. "They completed it in 1834 and it cost almost $3 million. Most of the canal system remains intact today and it's a reminder of the days when the delivery of freight depended upon a team of mules or steam tugboats. Thirty-six miles of the main canal and 22 miles of the feeder canal still exist, with many historic structures along its entire length."

"I've got to see this thing," said T-Bone. "Let's add it to the itinerary."

"Done," I said as I pushed away from the computer. "I think I should call my grandfather for this one."

"Good idea. I think your dad definitely needs a break."

My grandfather thought it sounded like a great trip. After checking the calendar of events, we planned to go on Saturday for the Mercer County 4-H Fair. The fair included 4-H animals and exhibits, food and homemade ice cream, hay rides, pony rides, music, farm tours, milking demonstrations, spinning, and children's crafts. Since we were new fans of 4-H, it was perfect.

When Saturday morning arrived, we were ready. We had bottles of water and comfortable shoes even though we weren't hiking to a bakery. It was a typical New Jersey summer day: hazy, hot, and humid. We started early to get a jump on the heat and so we could fit everything in.

94

"Have fun," my mom said as she gave me a kiss on the forehead. "And take it easy on your grandfather. It's going to be a hot one, and he's getting older."

"Mom, I hate to break it you," I laughed, "but he usually has more energy than us."

"Good point," she nodded. "Well, have a great day."

We headed north on Interstate 295 toward Trenton, where we drove left to Route 29. The sun was breaking through the haze reflecting on the Delaware River and I wondered how many people, over time, enjoyed this view. We went through a tunnel and T-Bone pointed to the words Historic Trenton at the entrance. As we glided past the *Trenton Makes Bridge* and the State House, I was happy Trenton still played a significant role in the state.

"Look at the sun shine on the gold dome of the State House," observed my grandfather. "It's such an important city that just needs some new ideas to reinvent itself."

"What would you do for Trenton?" asked T-Bone.

"Well, it's a little late for me to make such grandiose changes, but I would capitalize on Trenton's history, waterfront, and culture. You know, the state and federal buildings use one quarter of the city's land, so you have tens of thousands of people who come for work each day."

"That's good, right?" I asked.

"Well, it's half the battle," he smiled. "If I was in charge, I would turn Trenton into an historic gem. Trenton is the real deal; from the colonies to the revolution to the Industrial Revolution. It's real, it isn't fabricated. I'd use the Old Barracks and the Trent House to anchor a tourism program with re-enactors, taverns, tours, and shops. I'd give people a reason to visit and to stay after work."

"That's a good plan," said T-Bone. "What else?"

"Then," my grandfather continued, "I would develop the waterfront with artsy shops and restaurants with a giant walkway right over Route 29 to get there. Trenton doesn't need to invent a great environment; they simply need to develop the amazing assets they already have."

"Wow, you've given this some thought," I noticed.

"Your grandmother and I always love to solve the world's problems over our coffee," he laughed.

We continued on Route 29 and suddenly I noticed the canal on our left. It was conveniently tucked between the highway and the Delaware River and I imagined the laborers digging it with shovels. I couldn't imagine doing such back-breaking work every day and was glad they finished it before I was born. There was a very skinny bridge on our left that led to Washington Crossing, Pennsylvania. We pulled into Washington Crossing State Park and it hit me that this is where General Washington's troops made their very risky crossing.

We stopped by the Visitors Center and learned that the exhibit galleries explore the many facets of America's Revolutionary conflict with an emphasis on the military campaign known as "The Ten Crucial Days." The events of these ten days, December 25, 1776 through January 3, 1777, included the Continental Army's crossing of the Delaware River and the Battles of Trenton and Princeton.

We watched a short film about the war and checked out The Swan Collection, a living military history laboratory of the American Revolution with over 700 original objects from 1745 through 1789. It was an amazing place to get a feel for how important General Washington's time in Trenton was, not just for New Jersey, but for the United States of America. My grandfather joked that it was the last trick General Washington had up his sleeve to turn the tide of the war. He called it Washington's last-ditch effort. Besides the amazing history, the park had an Open Air Theater, an observatory, a nature center, trails, camping and a playground. There was also the Johnson Ferry House, an early 18th-century farmhouse and tavern near the Delaware River that was owned by Garret Johnson. He operated a 490-acre colonial plantation and a ferry service across the river in the 1700s. The house was probably used by General Washington and other officers at the time of the Christmas night crossing of the Delaware.

From there we went across the street to the D&R Canal State Park, the longest park in the state. There was a walking and biking path that went on for miles. We walked one segment and were relieved that there was enough shade to protect us from the sun, which was now peeking through the clouds. The trail was filled with joggers, couples walking and laughing, and families on bicycles. I made a note to come back with our bikes. My grandfather said it was considered one of the best family bike paths in the state.

We returned to the car and I asked my grandfather how long it would take to get to the Howell Farm. He told us it was about five miles from the park and we continued north along Route 29.

"I have a question," T-Bone announced. "Why do some of the signs say Daniel Bray Highway? Is this the Daniel Bray Highway or Route 29?"

"It said the John Fitch Way farther back," I added.

"You're both right," said my grandfather. "I've read my share of history books and many people who did less for this country have become more famous. Daniel Bray was a general in the army and played a pivotal role in many battles, including the Battle of Trenton."

"What did he do?" I asked.

"Well, with a few patriotic citizens he braved the enemy and collected enough boats from along the river to make the crossing of the icy Delaware by General Washington and his troops possible," he explained.

"How did you know that?" asked T-Bone.

"I did a little reading up before this trip," he said with a wink.

Poor Daniel Bray, I thought. Somehow he was left out of the history books. I wondered how many others had made huge contributions and never got the credit. *At least he got a highway.*

"What did John Fitch do?" I asked.

"He was a brass and silversmith as well as an inventor who served as a gunsmith during the Revolution."

My grandfather turned right on Pleasant Valley Road and we arrived at the Howell Living History Farm. I thought Inez and Charles Howell once lived there, but my grandfather said they rented it to tenant farmers and never lived there. The parking lot was crowded and the air was filled with excitement. Families pushing strollers, pulling wagons, and wearing babies were everywhere. There was so much to do that we weren't sure where to start.

We stumbled upon an odd contraption and a man dressed in farm clothes who was explaining that it was an ice cream machine. Not only were they making ice cream with something that looked like a motor for an old car, they were selling it as quick as they made it. We were planning to buy lunch first, but the heat of the afternoon sun changed the batting order to ice cream first, lunch second.

"This ice cream is incredible," I said. "It tastes different than ice cream we buy at the grocery store, but I can't think of a word to describe it."

"Fresh," said T-Bone, as he took another spoonful.

"Can't get it any fresher," my grandfather smiled.

We walked through the farm, stopping for demonstrations and checking out the 4-H animals. There were other kids proudly standing next to giant sheep who were about to be sheared and something called goat-carts. We couldn't resist and bought tickets for a ride in a cart pulled by a goat. There was a long line for the wagon rides, so we bought our tickets, played some old-fashioned games of chance, and grabbed some lunch. By the time we were finished, the line for the wagon ride was a bit shorter and we only had to wait ten minutes. Our driver told us the history of the farm and pointed out various points of interest as we clip-clopped along. The horses that pulled the wagon were enormous and when our ride was over, we got a picture with them. Thankfully, my grandfather didn't know how to turn the Flip Cam off and he captured the horse licking T-Bone's ear.

We stopped in the Visitors Center to see the winners of different craft and baking contests. The items looked so good that I reminded T-Bone, *twice*, that they weren't for sampling or for sale.

"So what do you think?" asked my grandfather.

"I think we should grab one more ice cream to toast Charles and Inez Howell," I suggested.

"Perfect," he agreed. "Without their generosity, this would probably be condos or a shopping center."

"What?" T-Bone quickly turned to ask. "How could anyone turn this farm into a shopping center?"

"Well, historic landmarks and places of importance can only be preserved if they're appreciated. Mrs. Howell knew that this farm would be appreciated as a great way to travel in time, so to speak, while reminding folks about the importance of agriculture. It's only when people stop paying attention, places like this face danger."

"Do you really think this farm would have been sold to someone to build houses or shops?" I asked.

.

"There's a good chance," he said. "That's why it's so important for people with means to be generous and the rest of us to take advantage of these great resources. Call me old-fashioned, but families shouldn't spend the weekends around the house or doing separate things; this is what they should be doing: spending time together, learning about an amazing state, and spending money right here, which helps our economy. Geesh, I'm starting to sound like you guys!"

"You *are* starting to sound like us. And by means, do you mean money?" asked T-Bone.

"That's exactly what I mean," he answered.

"Then I'm going to make a lot of money," said T-Bone. "So I can be a philosophist."

"You mean philanthropist," my grandfather laughed.

"Sure," said T-Bone, "that, too!"

When we left the farm, I assumed we were going home, as I had nothing left on the itinerary. My grandfather had a different plan. We continued north on what we decided to call the Route 29-Daniel Bray-John-Fitch Highway to a town called Lambertville, only 3 miles north. Just like Washington Crossing, New Jersey, it was also connected to Pennsylvania by a very, very skinny bridge. It was a warm Saturday night and the town was bustling. We parked by the Lambertville Station and started walking.

Lambertville reminded me of pictures of New England towns. Set along the river, the streets were lined with trees and church steeples, and the shops and homes were, as my mom would say, meticulous. My grandfather pointed out numerous art galleries, bed and breakfast inns, and the huge Lambertville Station hotel.

"What's on the other side?" asked T-Bone.

"That's New Hope, Pennsylvania."

"Do you think we could walk over the bridge?" I asked.

"Absolutely," said my grandfather. "Let's have dinner first and then we can walk it off on the bridge."

"I don't know about that," T-Bone hesitated. "Should we really cross over to Pennsylvania? You know, being New Jersey's ambassadors and all?"

"They're our neighbors, not our enemies," I laughed as we headed toward the restaurant. "I think it'll be okay."

My grandfather took us to a place called Rick's, an Italian restaurant with red and white checkered tablecloths. It smelled amazing before we walked in and even better once we sat down. T-Bone and I both ordered cheese ravioli and meatballs. My grandfather must have worked up an appetite because he ordered a soup, salad, and shrimp over linguine. It was delicious and we definitely needed to walk across that bridge when we were finished.

"Thanks, this was great," T-Bone said to my grandfather.

"Yeah, thanks for bringing us."

"Boys, I should be thanking you. I have thoroughly enjoyed each trip we have taken. I get to spend time with you both, see great places, and feel young again."

"Young again?" T-Bone laughed. "You have more energy than both of us put together. I know you're a grandfather, but you don't seem nearly as old as you are."

"Tommy, I'm going to *choose* to take that as a compliment," he said as he threw his napkin on his plate. "And then I'm going to take a walk. You boys ready?"

We got up and checked out the stores while my grandfather told us a little about the town. Once busy with mills, the railroad, and the canal traffic, Lambertville was now considered the Antique Capital of New Jersey. When times and industries changed, it re-invented itself along the river. It was a great example for other cities and towns facing those same kinds of changes.

We took our much-needed stroll across the bridge to Pennsylvania and walked around New Hope for a little while. My grandfather pointed out the Bucks County Playhouse where he used to take my grandmother to see plays like *Bye-Bye Birdie* and *Oklahoma*.

"That's not a bad idea," said T-Bone.

"What isn't?" I asked.

"Someone wrote a play called *Oklahoma*," he shrugged. "So I'm gonna write a play called *New Jersey*. But it won't be the things people think they know about our state from rumors and television shows. It'll be real and show people what a great state this is."

"You should," my grandfather agreed. "You'd make the best wealthy, philanthropist, 4-H playwright in the world."

When we returned to Lambertville, we appreciated just how wide the Delaware River was at that point and we had even more respect for General Washington and his troops. We were tired and it was a beautiful summer night. I couldn't imagine crossing that icy river in a blizzard. Before we left, my grandfather informed us that he felt like a cup of coffee. I couldn't believe he was still going.

We arrived at the Lambertville Station, a restored 19th-century train station with great views of the water. We sat at the Canal Side outdoor tables, and while my grandfather enjoyed his coffee, we ordered dessert. He told us the Delaware River was also very popular for water sports such as kayaking and tubing.

"People float down the river in a tube?" asked T-Bone.

"Absolutely," he explained. "You can go to Delaware River Tubing or Bucks County River Country and float down the river as a family."

"Is it safe?" I asked.

"Very," he replied. "And you can even eat lunch at the Famous River Hot Dog Man."

"That's funny," laughed T-Bone. "When you say it like that, it sounds like he's in the river."

"He is," my grandfather smiled.

"Seriously?" asked T-Bone. "Sign me up. Nick, you in?"

"Hot dogs in a river?" I said. "Who wouldn't be in?"

It was ironic that when people thought about water and New Jersey, the first thing that came to mind was the Atlantic Ocean. But, as my grandfather told us while he sipped his coffee, New Jersey has almost 700 square miles of water with over 100 rivers and creeks and over 800 lakes and ponds.

"That's a lot of water," said T-Bone. "Especially for one Famous River Hot Dog Man to cover."

"If you really want to be impressed, read about the Cohansey Aquifilter, under the Pine Barrens. It contains over 17 trillion gallons of fresh water.

"Good thing that water's underground," T-Bone remarked. "That would make some huge puddles."

"Puddles?" said my grandfather. "That's enough to cover the entire state with 10 feet of water."

Wow, I thought, 17 trillion gallons of fresh water and a Famous River Hot Dog Man all in one state. What's better than that?

Chapter Eight

The next morning, I decided to sleep in. Saturday's day trip was exhausting and I could have slept all day. I woke up a couple of times and fell back to sleep. I decided to sleep until lunch, eat, and then take a nap until dinner. After that, I'd play it by car, but I was leaning toward going to bed early. These trips were catching up with me.

I looked at the clock and it was eight thirty. I pulled the covers over my head, hoping I could jump back into the dream I was having. I was squinting, trying to force myself back to sleep, but no dice. The harder I tried, the more I woke up and the less I remembered. Before I could try again, I heard my bedroom door opening. I was hoping it wasn't my sisters and surprisingly, it was my dad.

"Nick, wake up," he said as he tapped my shoulder.

I opened one eye and asked him what was going on. "We're going on another day trip," he smiled.

"You do realize that we're the junior ambassadors, right?"

"Sure," he said, "but you do realize that we're the people

who introduced you and Tommy to the New Jersey day trip, right? We, as in your mother and I, created the first Garden State Adventures you two took."

He had a point. It really was the first seven day trips that started this passion for seeing every inch of New Jersey and telling other kids about what we saw. Still, I had become quite the trip planner and wasn't sure what I would do if my dad's itinerary wasn't good.

"So," he continued, "we typed up an itinerary, using your format. Check it out and let me know if you want to do it. It's totally up to you. You're the ambassador. You make the call. It's all up to you. But just hurry because Tommy's downstairs and we're leaving in ten minutes."

"Then why did you say it was all up to me?"

"Just being polite," he said as he handed me the itinerary and winked. "And seriously, hurry up."

So much for my Sunday of sleeping and eating, I thought. I stayed under the covers for a few minutes and then realized that he had left the itinerary on my bed. I reached over and gave it a glance. I hated to admit it, but it wasn't bad. He included something for everyone, ample time for breaks, and a list of substitutions in case a location was closed, as well as possible places to eat. Then he wrote the hours of operation in the margin of the paper along with prices and phone numbers. The only thing I couldn't figure out was where we were going. My dad used abbreviations for everything, so I had no idea where we would end up and I was too tired to try to guess. When I went downstairs, everyone was ready and waiting for me.

"Hey, look, it's *sleepy beauty,*" said T-Bone.

"Aren't you tired?" I asked in between yawns.

"Never too tired to explore New Jersey," he answered. "When your mom called this morning, I ran right over."

"I'm sure you did," I shook my head, hoping no one would speak to me before I really had a chance to wake up.

Once I sat down in the van, I grabbed the atlas and used the abbreviations to try to figure out where we were going. We were headed north, so that eliminated half of the state. We were on Route 206 and I kept following our route with the atlas. As we passed Princeton, my finger glided over Montgomery, Belle Mead, Hillsborough, and Somerville. I noticed the towns were much more rural. I wondered why we hadn't turned onto a highway yet.

"Hey, Dad, are you lost?" I asked.

"Nice try," he smirked. "You're just trying to get me to tell you where we're going."

"No, seriously," I said. "I was just curious why you haven't turned onto a highway yet. This road has an awful lot of lights, don't you think?"

"You in a hurry?" he asked, totally not taking the bait.

"No," I shook my head. "I was just curious."

"You know, this is what families used to do on Sundays," said my mom. "You would get in the car and drive the scenic routes."

"You nailed it," I laughed. "This is definitely the scenic route. Did you add this much travel time to the itinerary?"

"You know, this isn't our first time on the tour," my dad replied. "Relax, and soak in the scenery."

"Hey, where did Route 202 come from?" asked T-Bone. "I thought we were on Route 206."

"Sometimes roads overlap, or they have both a number and a name," said my mom. "Or the name of a road changes as the road extends into another town."

"Like the Route 29-Daniel Bray-John Fitch Way?" I asked.

"Sure," my mom smiled, not getting the reference and unsure of who Daniel Bray and John Fitch even were.

We continued our journey north and drove through Bedminster, Peapack and Gladstone, and then Chester. When we stopped at the light in Chester, I recognized the large white restaurant ahead that looked different.

"Mom, what happened?" I asked.

"What do you mean?"

"I mean, last time we were here, that restaurant was Larison's Turkey Farm. What happened?"

"Hard to know," my dad explained. "It could have been the economy, competition, or a decision to retire. Either way, it's a shame when a popular, established business is no longer there."

"You're right," my mom agreed. "I really enjoyed that restaurant. It felt like Thanksgiving, no matter what time of year."

"So where are we going?" I said, hoping I would catch my dad off guard.

"Straight," he said, glancing at me through the mirror.

"Hold on, are we going back to Wild West City?" I asked, confident that I had figured it out. According to the map, we were getting close to Netcong and my dad and T-Bone had been so excited about the rodeo and the horse park. It all made sense, *except for the fact that I was wrong*. While my dad's silence didn't confirm that I was wrong, driving through Flanders, Netcong, Stanhope and Allamuchy did. Seeing Wild West City would have required making a right at the fork in the road. We drove left.

"Look at the name of that town," said T-Bone as he pointed to a sign. "What does Allamuchy mean?"

"I've got that right here," said my mom, paging through a notebook. "Before Allamuchy was a town, it was a Lenni-Lenape village and the name meant *a place in the hills*. Quaker families migrated to the area from Europe around 1745. The Quakers, also known as the "Society of Friends," were the first "white" settlers in the area. They built a school called Quaker Grove School, which was used until the 1930s. The settlement even became a station for the Underground Railroad during the Civil War."

"Like the Wheaton Pharmacy in the City of Burlington?" I remembered. "Mayor Jim told us they were a stop on the Underground Railroad, too."

"Exactly," she said.

"What else do they have there?" asked T-Bone.

"Before I tell you what they *have*, let me tell you what they *had*," she read. "By 1886, Allamuchy had 28 houses, two stores, a blacksmith, a wheelwright shop, a post office, a hotel, two grist mills and a creamery."

"Wow, 28 houses isn't much, is it?" I said.

"Now, they have about 4,000 residents," she read. Then she had my dad drive by a place called the Villa Madonna Mansion. It was a huge mansion: 18,000 square feet, 23 rooms, and it sat on 32 acres of land next to the Allamuchy Pond and the State Park. Winthrop Rutherford constructed the estate in 1903 and married Lucy Mercer in 1920. When she died, she donated the estate to the Catholic sisters as a retirement home. Now the estate is part of the Allamuchy School District and it houses a K-2 school.

It was a really pretty town and I was sure that the people who made jokes about New Jersey had never been to this town before. It was another example of how diverse the Garden State was. Allamuchy wasn't filled with shopping centers and movie theaters; instead there were mountains, lakes, hiking, fishing, biking, bird watching, swimming, horseback riding, and several other outdoor activities to enjoy. It was hard to believe, but one-third of the township was actually the Allamuchy State Park.

After our mini tour of the park, we continued our journey, although I still had no idea where our final destination would be. My dad continued north on Route 206 through Byram, Andover, and Newton. The area felt very familiar and then I remembered visiting the Newton Fire Museum on our High Point day trip. We finally turned right onto Plains Road and soon it was all clear.

"Okay, guys," my mom said, "we're here!"

"Where's here?" asked T-Bone.

"We're at the New Jersey State Fair! Do you believe it?" she gushed.

It was an amazing sight. There were tents everywhere in the middle of nowhere. We were at the Sussex County Fairgrounds and the fair was enormous. We were starving and they sold every kind of food you could imagine. We had sausage sandwiches, fries, lemonade, and corn.

"Now that we've had lunch," my mom suggested, "we'll wait a little while to get snacks."

"That's a plan, Mrs. A," T-Bone agreed. "Hey, look at that, people are heading to that tent."

"Let's go!" My dad hoisted Emma onto his shoulders.

"Me, too," said Maggie, not grasping the fact that my dad only had one set of shoulders.

"Race you to the tent," said Timmy, trying to distract her.

"Last one there is a rotten egg," T-Bone yelled and took off. While Timmy held back to let Maggie win, T-Bone, in an attempt to beat anyone in a foot race, flew by at top speed. We all just looked at one another.

"Where did you find him?" My dad shook his head.

"New Jersey," I laughed, "which was *your idea*."

We entered the tent in time to find seats on the bleachers for the magic show. We sat next to a family with two little girls. While all of the kids were excited by the tricks, no one was more excited than T-Bone. Every time the magician performed a trick, T-Bone yelled, "Bravo!" Every time he yelled, the family next to us turned our way.

"It's okay," I said to them, "he loves magic."

"Me, too," said the younger girl with a great big smile. "Is he a magician?"

"Who? T-Bone?" I laughed. "The only thing he makes disappear is food."

"His name is funny," she said.

"His real name is Tommy," I explained. "That's just his nickname."

"Why do they call him telephone?" she asked.

"No, no," I laughed. "It's T-Bone, not telephone."

"Oh," she nodded. "My name is Ava and my sister is Grace. I don't think we have nicknames. Hold on...Mom, do we have nicknames?"

"Not as cool as T-Bone," her mom laughed.

We watched the magic show and we watched T-Bone watching the magic show. He was as entertaining as the show. When it was over, we checked out the Fun Barn, which was a tent set up for younger kids. My sisters dug for potatoes, played with very realistic fake food on a conveyor belt, and built a scarecrow. T-Bone said he would help them, but he really just needed a reason to play.

When we left the Fun Barn, we headed to the Piglet Race. This was probably one of the funniest things I had ever seen. As we were cheering for the pigs I noticed Grace and Ava were also watching with their family. T-Bone ran up to them and told them to check out the Fun Barn. They seemed excited that T-Bone remembered them and they suggested he climb a coconut tree. I thought that was their polite way of telling him to get lost, but it turned out there really was a rock wall shaped like a coconut tree.

"This place is awesome," said T-Bone. "We should come here every week."

"That's a great idea," my dad sarcastically agreed, "except that it's an annual ten day fair."

"Then we should come all ten-days," he decided.

"Yeah, *you* should," said my dad, stressing the *you* instead of the *we*.

As we continued exploring the fair, we found funnel cake, snow cones, and candy apples. T-Bone, Timmy, and I rode elephants while my sisters rode donkeys. When we were through, we checked out the honey bee exhibit, the petting zoo, and the 4-H tent. The 4-H tent was really cool. Kids were there, showing every kind of farm animal: goats, poultry, cows, livestock, and even baby chicks. Before we headed back to the car my mom insisted on checking out the vendors. My mom always admired handmade quilts and was thrilled when my dad bought one.

"What about the rides?" asked Maggie. "I see rides. They're right there. See, I see them. Do you see them?"

"I do see them," said my mom, "but we spent a lot of money and I think we'll have to go on them another time."

"Great! When?" asked T-Bone.

"A-noth-er day," my mom said, making the T-Bone-I'm-just-saying-that face.

When we returned to the car, we were all exhausted. I assumed we were heading back home, but I was wrong. The only thing my parents loved more than going on a good New Jersey day trip was planning a good New Jersey day trip. Whatever it was, they were sure having fun keeping the details a secret.

"Our next stop," declared my mom, "will be Rockaway."

"Is it a music town?" asked Timmy.

"Yeah, they shortened the original name from Rock-the-night-away to Rockaway," I sarcastically answered.

"Cool," said T-Bone. "I love music."

"I'm joking," I said as I rolled my eyes. "It's probably because they had so many rocks to move out of the way."

"You're both wrong," Maggie chimed in. "It's the song mommy always singed to us: Rockaway baby in the treetop."

"They're all very creative ideas," said my mom, "but they're also wrong. In 1715, Dutch settlers gave it that name based on the Indian word *Rechouwakie* meaning the place of sands. Rockaway was the first district in America to actively work and mine iron ore. The contribution of the iron industry assisted in the cause for independence from England."

"Did they have a furnace like Allaire State Park?" I asked.

"Actually, around 1776, Morris County was the main smelting center of the United States. Rockaway Township had several forges and three blast furnaces were located in Hibernia, Mount Hope and Split Rock. The Split Rock furnace, the only one still standing, is located below the dam of the Split Rock Reservoir."

"Can we see it?" asked T-Bone.

"If we can find it," my mom laughed, then continued. "The forges and furnaces at Hibernia and Mount Hope furnished the Continental Army with shovels, axes, cannons, cannonballs, grapeshot, and other supplies."

"Did the soldiers work there?" I asked, knowing most men were in the army.

"Well, I read on the Rockaway Library's website that even though there was a desperate need for soldiers in the Continental Army, the New Jersey Legislature adopted a resolution on October 7, 1777, exempting fifty men at Mount Hope and twenty-five men at Hibernia from entering military service. These men were needed to mine the iron and produce the equipment needed for battle."

"So even though they weren't fighting, they were helping the soldiers?" I asked.

"Absolutely," said my dad. "The soldiers needed those supplies, and this township was really an important part of the effort for the whole country."

"We better watch our backs, Nick," T-Bone laughed. "I think your parents want our ambassador jobs."

"Wouldn't dream of it," my mom smiled. "Think of it this way; you didn't just get other families excited about exploring New Jersey; we caught the bug, too."

"Get it out! Get the bug out of the car," yelled Maggie, still not a fan of bugs. "I hate bugs! Get rid of the bug!"

While we explained to my sister that catching a bug was an expression, my dad had arrived. We found the Split Rock Reservoir and then spotted the furnace. My mom

119

told us that when the industry slowed down, they built the Morris Canal, a significant engineering design, and the Rockaway Village came back to life. I wondered if they used Irish immigrants like they did on the Delaware & Raritan Canal. My mom told us it was private investors that built it, not the state. The canal was important at a time when communities were separated by land obstacles and when shipping goods on land was slow and expensive. It turned out that it was much easier and less expensive to have a couple of mules to pull barges down a canal.

"Will we get to see the mule barges?" asked T-Bone.

"If you have a time machine," my dad laughed. "You see, the canals filled a need and were a milestone of progress. But progress is always moving forward. When you solve one problem or improve a situation, other things become obsolete."

"You mean like when they invented crazy straws?" asked Timmy.

"What?" asked my dad.

"You know, there were straight straws and then they invented crazy straws with all kinds of loops."

"No," my dad shook his head, "that's not a great example because we still use straight straws. In fact, how often do you see people using a crazy straw?"

"Not nearly enough," he shrugged.

"Boys, think of it this way," my mom began, "once upon a time, people used a wash bucket and washboard to clean their clothes. Well, when the automatic washing machine was invented, the need for wash buckets and washboards dropped off until people no longer used them."

"Oh, you mean like musical instruments?" asked T-Bone.

"Instruments?" replied my dad. "How do you figure?"

"Now you can play instruments with apps, or even better, with music video games," he explained.

"No," my dad shook his head. "I don't quite think music apps and video games will ever replace real instruments."

"So anyway," said my mom, "just like the canals replaced wagons, trains replaced the canals."

"It's kind of sad," I said. "You build this canal and then before you know it, no one needs it."

"Progress," my dad nodded. "It's all about progress."

We drove over the reservoir and across the dam along a skinny concrete bridge with chain link fences on each side and a guard shack at the center. On the other side, I saw the stone furnace and assumed most people drove by without paying much attention to it. As years passed, it would probably be forgotten, although I hoped not. My mom told us this was one of the most beautiful lakes in the state and that the reservoir was actually several large, interconnected lakes with many large islands. It was very popular with fishermen, kayakers, and hikers, and I could see why.

It was starting to get late and, despite eating our way through the New Jersey State Fair, we were getting hungry again. On our way to Route 80, we came upon the Hibernia Diner and decided to get a late dinner. I was always excited when we ate at diners; the menus had so many choices and they always gave you so much food. At home, my mom was always talking about healthy portions, but when we ate at a diner, she enjoyed those giant plates over-filled with food. We usually only ate half and this meant she wouldn't have to cook the next night. Before we made our selections, she would always tell us to order something we'd feel like eating the next day. There was definitely a method to her madness.

As predicted, our meals were huge and, more importantly, they were delicious. When our server offered us dessert, we all smiled and politely declined. Between the fair and our dinner, we couldn't eat another bite. It was getting late and we decided it was time to head home.

"Hey, Dad," said Timmy as he buckled his seat belt, "I think I want to be a 4-H kid."

"That's great," my dad answered. "We can look into it."

"I wanna show goats," he continued.

"Show them what?" asked T-Bone. "What could *you* possibly teach a goat?"

"You could teach them to tap dance," Maggie suggested.

"That wouldn't work," said T-Bone. "Timmy would need to know how to tap dance."

"Sure, *that's* why it wouldn't work," said my dad.

"Do you know how to jump hurdles?" T-Bone continued.

"I just want to keep them in our yard and win ribbons," said Timmy. "I don't want to teach goats how to dance."

"That's good," my mom laughed, "although I'm pretty sure there are rules about raising goats in residential areas. But don't worry, they have lots of fun things to try. I think it's a great idea."

I wasn't one hundred percent sure that our town had rules about having a goat in our yard, but I was one hundred percent sure *that my parents did*.

Chapter Nine

As much as I wanted to plan another day trip, I realized we needed to write some of our reports. I never enjoyed writing until I started writing about our trips. Writing it down was the closest thing to going back to those places. As soon as T-Bone arrived, we began.

"You know we were invited to Historic Cold Spring Village," he said, although I was trying to forget.

"Oh, yeah," I mumbled and nodded my head.

"So I think we should call Annie and find out when she wants us to speak," he suggested.

"Maybe we should wait for her to call us. We don't want to seem pushy, do we?"

"No, not at all," T-Bone replied. "But I think she's looking forward to our visit."

There was no way around it. It was inevitable. As much as I loved Historic Cold Spring Village, I was still terrified to speak in public. I'd have been thrilled to tour the village, eat at the Grange Restaurant, and listen to T-Bone give a speech. Unfortunately, that wasn't happening.

It took about three hours to write our reports and get our pictures downloaded. During that time T-Bone excitedly discussed what we should talk about when we visited Cold Spring Village.

"Okay, that's it," I said, grabbing our reports and memory stick. "Let's see if my mom can drive us to Trenton."

My mom was happy to bring us and my dad was happy to stay home. Clearly, he didn't have my mother's stamina.

"Wow, it's almost lunchtime," T-Bone tried to be subtle.

"Is that so?" she asked.

"It is so," he replied. "Do they have any historic taverns in Trenton? I'm in the mood for old."

"Old?" my mom asked. "I might have something for you."

"Have we ever been there?" I asked.

"No, but I read about this place in the newspaper recently and thought about trying it," she explained. "It's in the Chambersburg section of the city."

We drove down Chambers Street and turned onto Roebling Avenue. T-Bone and I immediately made the Roebling-family connection and we already felt the history. We walked into a place called Papa's Tomato Pies with a large, red awning and a stained glass window with the letter *P*. It wasn't very big, had long wooden booths on each side, and walls covered with picture collages. A waitress told us we could sit wherever we liked, so we sat near the kitchen. My mom ordered a large tomato pie with half sausage and half meatball and a pitcher of red cream soda.

"So what gives?" asked T-Bone. "This place smells great, but I don't think George Washington ate here."

"True," my mom nodded. "George Washington definitely did not eat here, but this place is very historic."

"What is it, the oldest pizza place in New Jersey?" T-Bone sarcastically asked.

"Actually," said my mom, pointing to a sign behind us, "it's the oldest pizza restaurant in the country."

"What?" T-Bone asked. "Are you serious, Mrs. A.? Because if you are, then that's some very cool history."

"Says so right there," she gestured with her head. "I read in the paper that it's the longest continuously operating pizza restaurant in the country. There was a dispute with a restaurant in New York that opened earlier, though."

"Hold on," T-Bone interrupted. "Then that means they're not the oldest."

"This is why you have to read the whole article," my mom smirked. "The restaurant that opened first closed for several years, so they weren't open continuously."

"So this is the oldest pizza place in the whole country that never closed?" I tried to confirm.

"That's right," said a man who was wiping the table behind us. "I'm Nick Azzaro and you are sitting in the oldest pizza restaurant in the country."

"Did you start the restaurant?" asked T-Bone.

"No," he laughed. "My grandfather, Joe Papa, started it. My father, Dominik, who everyone calls Abbie, married Joe's daughter, Tessie. They were the second generation. I'm the third generation, and my son, Donnie, is the fourth."

"Wow," I said. "When did they open?"

"In 1912," said Nick, "and it's been a family business ever since. Before the machines, my grandfather made his dough by hand and taught pie-making to many pie-makers who went on to have their own businesses in the area."

"I read a nice article about your restaurant in the paper," said my mom. "That's quite an achievement."

"Thank you," he said. "And thanks for stopping by."

"Our pleasure," said T-Bone as he sipped the red cream

soda. "This stuff is great. They oughta bottle it."

"They do," my mom laughed.

The tomato pie tasted as good as it smelled and we all sampled both sides: meatball and sausage. I wondered how long they would keep going. With tomato pie that good, I figured it would be a long time. My mom thought we'd have a lot left over for my dad to try, but there were only two slices left. I figured he would be lucky if those actually made it home.

We headed to the State House and ran inside. The security guard knew who we were and called Billy to come out and meet us. We told him about the places we had selected and he told us about Tessy Colegrove.

"We know," said T-Bone.

"What?" he asked. "How could you possibly know?"

"We met Tessy at the Stewart's Root Beer restaurant in Long Branch," T-Bone answered matter-of-factly.

"Are you serious?" he asked in disbelief. "You didn't know her and you just bumped into her?"

"Pretty much," I said. "You know, it's a small world!"

"Wow, you kids really do get around," he laughed. "So do you think you're going to head up to the bakery?"

"Not only are we going," said T-Bone, "Tessy's mom said we won't even have to wait in line."

"So when are you going?"

"That depends on my mom," I shrugged.

"Well, I was going to surprise you," she said, "but I talked to Lisa Valastro and we set up a visit for tomorrow."

"Yes!" I yelled and started to high-five T-Bone. I was shocked when he left me hanging and didn't even raise his hand. "What's with you?"

"I wish your mom would have told me before I ate all of that pizza," he sulked.

"Don't worry, Tommy," my mom winked. "I have faith that you can still put away a fair share of baked goods."

"That's true," he conceded. "Plus, I can take some home. I think the key will be pacing myself."

"Remember, it's not a race; it's a marathon," Billy laughed as he thanked us and headed back to work.

We decided to leave for Hoboken early the next morning and make a day trip out of it. My mom suggested 8:00. T-Bone arrived at 6:00. When the doorbell rang, everyone knew who it would be, so I staggered down the stairs to answer it.

"Give me a C," T-Bone attempted to start a cheer. I just stared at him. "Okay, I'll answer myself, C."

"Do you know what time it is?" I asked, ignoring his cheer.

"Give me an A," he continued, despite my silence. "Okay, I'll do that one myself, A."

"Seriously," I said. "Are you really this excited?"

"Give me an R," he cheered alone. "R. Give me an L. L. Give me an O. O."

Suddenly he stopped and looked up. I wasn't sure what he was doing, but then I had a pretty good idea. "You forgot the next letter, didn't you?" I said, shaking my head.

"I wouldn't say forgot; it's more like lost my place in all of the excitement."

"What excitement?" I asked. "You're still standing in my not-very-exciting foyer at six o'clock in the morning."

He continued staring at me.

"Okay," I relented. "S."

"Thanks," he bowed his head. "Now, give me an S."

"S," I said, hoping if I answered, I could turn on the television for him and go back to sleep.

"What's it spell?" he asked.

"You really don't know, do you?" I said.

"Very funny," he squinted, "but since you refuse to play, I'll answer it myself. What's it spell? Cake Boss!"

"You know you spelled C-A-R-L-O-S, right?"

"Oh, that's right," he said. "Carlo's!"

"Do you want to watch something while I go back to sleep?" I asked.

"Yeah, right," he laughed. "You're watching with me."

"Watching what?"

"This," he said, taking out the Cake Boss DVDs. "We don't have time to watch them all, but you need to know who everybody is so you don't look stupid."

"You don't want *me* to look stupid?" I asked. T-Bone was wearing a Cake Boss t-shirt, a chef's hat, and he had a whisk dangling from his belt loop. And he was worried about *me* looking stupid? "What's with the chef hat and the whisk?"

"You know, you can never be too prepared," he explained. "What if I'm standing there and Mama asks me to stir something for her? Then what?"

"I'm pretty sure they don't invite visitors to stir food and furthermore, if they did, they'd give you a whisk."

"Amateur," T-Bone laughed as he turned the DVD on in our family room.

I sat down and started watching the show. Before I knew it, we were laughing hysterically. We must have been louder than I thought because halfway through the first episode, my parents were standing with their arms crossed. I thought I was in trouble, but they started laughing, too.

My parents laughed so loud, Timmy and my sisters woke up and came down. T-Bone was our Cake Boss tour guide and he fast-forwarded to his favorite parts, his favorite cakes, and his favorite pranks, always stopping when Mama came on. In about an hour and a half we had all become Valastro family experts.

"So this is where we're going today?" asked my dad. "And more importantly, do they know we're bringing Tommy?"

"Yes, and sure do," T-Bone confirmed.

When the Cake Boss marathon was over, we all got ready. I ran in the kitchen and tied a spatula and a wooden spoon to my belt loop. I walked by T-Bone and waited for him to notice.

"Hey, Nick, what are you doing?"

"Just wanna be prepared for when they ask me to cook."

"That's great," he said nervously. "But they bake at the ba-ker-y, they don't cook. It's like bringing a catcher's mitt to a basketball game. You're bringing the wrong tools. You better grab a measuring cup."

"I'm not bringing anything," I laughed as I untied them and brought them back to the kitchen.

"Good," he said with a sigh of relief, "if you showed up with those tools, you'd look ridiculous."

We took the turnpike north and headed to Hoboken. I remembered Hoboken was the sight of the first-ever baseball game at the Elysian Fields between the New York Nine and the Knickerbockers. Being a huge baseball fan, I always thought that was one of New Jersey's best firsts and Hoboken owned it.

"Let's go to Washington Street," my mom suggested. "Then I can give you the real tour."

"Have you been here?" I asked.

"No, I just went on www.hobokennj.org and did my homework," she answered.

"Shouldn't we go to the bakery now?" asked T-Bone, growing more impatient by the moment.

"We will, we will," my mom laughed. "I told Lisa we would check out the town first and then meet her at the bakery at 3:00."

"3:00?" T-Bone asked in horror. "Are you serious? That won't leave us time to bake anything."

"Don't worry," said my dad. "I'm sure they're good."

It took a few minutes to convince T-Bone that touring Hoboken would not interfere with touring Carlo's Bakery. We told him it would help him make great small talk. After all, he couldn't just tell them who they were all day. My mom told us a little about Hoboken while we drove through the parking garage. She said that in 1783, the "island" was purchased by Colonel John Stevens for about $100,000 by today's standards. In 1820, he transformed the wild, but beautiful waterfront into a resort. He created a path called River Walk, which ran along the waterfront to what were then the Elysian Fields. Located at the mouth of New York Harbor, piers for passengers and freight quickly grew along the waterfront. The city prospered as a major trans-Atlantic port. In 1907, the Erie-Lackawanna Terminal was built to replace the original terminal, which was destroyed by fire. A registered historic site, the terminal served commuter ferries to New York City and trains traveling west. In 1908, the first subway train linking the terminal and Manhattan opened at the site.

"So the Stevens family was to Hoboken as the Kusers and Roeblings were to Trenton?" I asked.

"Pretty much," said my mom. "The website said that the Stevens family founded churches and schools, and in 1870 the Stevens Institute of Technology was founded with a land grant donated by Edwin A. Stevens. The Stevens gatehouse, built in 1859, survives the Stevens Castle, a magnificent 34-room family mansion which topped the bluff until its demolition in 1959."

"Not again," said T-Bone.

"What's he talking about?" asked my dad.

"He has a hard time letting go of historic houses."

"Even if they're not his and he's never seen them?"

"Especially those," I laughed.

"Hey, do you think Colonel Stevens knew Colonel Kuser?" asked T-Bone, noting the similarities of both men: they were both called colonel, they were both rich, and they both had mansions that were destroyed. It was a good theory, until my mom told us that Colonel John Stevens was born in 1749 and was a real Colonel, starting as a captain in George Washington's army and then collecting taxes as the Treasurer of New Jersey. Colonel Anthony Kuser was born in 1862 and, even though they both came from prominent families, Colonel was a nickname for him. So I figured they didn't run in the same circles, especially since John Stevens died before Anthony Kuser was born. Slightly disappointed by that revelation, T-Bone regrouped as we entered daylight from the dark parking garage. We walked along the Hudson River Waterfront Walkway and realized New Jersey has even better views than New York. After all, we got to admire their amazing skyline and they had to come to New Jersey to see it. We stopped by the Pier A Park and learned it was one of the nation's Top Ten Urban Parks. We agreed and assumed the hundreds of sunbathers did, too.

We were excited to be in Hoboken and excited to visit Carlo's Bake Shop. My mom sensed our excitement and walked us over to Washington Street.

"Are you bringing us early? Are you bringing us early?" asked T-Bone. "Please say you're bringing us early."

"Sorry," my mom said with a slightly sad face. "We figured we'd check out Washington Street for a little while and then get something to eat first."

"Not me," said T-Bone. "I've hardly even had any liquid today, so I'm definitely not using precious stomach space on regular food."

"Perfect," said my Dad. "Let's eat."

We went to a place called Tutta Pasta and sat outside. From this highly recommended restaurant, we could see the line at Carlo's Bake Shop down the street. It was almost pitiful, watching T-Bone watch the line. It was like his body was sitting at our table in the restaurant, but his mind wasn't. His mind was inside the bakery, sitting at a table with Tessy, Lisa, John, Lucia, and Mama, filling cannoli shells and stirring something with his whisk.

I remembered Washington Street from the last time my parents brought us to Hoboken. As an ambassador, I was paying much more attention this time. Last time we ate at Amanda's Restaurant, and I remember my dad saying how much he enjoyed it. Of course he did, I thought, the food was awesome and T-Bone paid for it with the money he won on the radio. As we sat outside and ate our dinner, T-Bone finally ordered a cup of soup. Our meals were great and we were anxious to head over to the bakery.

"There's another one." T-Bone rested his head on the table.

"Another what?" I asked.

"Another happy customer from Carlo's Bake Shop," he pointed. "That's the sixth person to walk in with boxes from the bakery."

"Is that a problem?" asked my dad.

"If they're taking the last lobster tail or cannoli, then yes it is," T-Bone replied.

We thought it was funny how serious T-Bone was about the visit. While he played with the whisk, I hoped it was everything he thought it would be. Most importantly, I hoped Mama was there. I really hoped Mama was there.

When we left Tutta Pasta, we had two great big bags of leftovers. Apparently, T-Bone had everyone thinking about saving room for dessert. We saw the line in front of the bakery that stretched out front and then continued across the street. It was just like T-Bone predicted.

We approached the door and encountered a doorman with a headset on.

"How are you?" he asked.

"We're here," said T-Bone. "We're finally here."

Oh, no, I thought, his tongue must be swelling.

"Hi, we're here to see Lisa and Tessy," said my mom.

"Nicky, T-Bone, and family?" asked the doorman.

"We're here," said T-Bone.

"That's us," said my dad, moving T-Bone out of the way. He opened the door and it was amazing. The aroma was overwhelming. There was no doubt that this was the best-smelling building ever. There were so many customers and fans in front of the counter; they were at least twelve deep. It seemed like there were as many employees, too. As the doorman led us behind the counter, everyone's attention turned in our direction. I heard people asking each other who we were, wondering if we were celebrities. Halfway through the counter area, Lisa Valastro started heading in our direction. As soon as the first customer spotted her, the place went wild. She was very gracious: smiling, waving, and stopping for pictures along the way. Customers were calling her name from every direction and I think we ended up in a lot of just-in-case pictures: people taking pictures of us, just in case we were famous.

"Hi, everyone," Lisa greeted us with a big smile. "Welcome to Carlo's Bake Shop."

"Hi, Lisa," I said, pretty sure T-Bone was on the verge of fainting. "Thanks for not making us wait in line."

"You're welcome," she smiled. "Let me get the kids."

As she turned to call the kids, I turned to look at T-Bone. His eyes were glazed over and his mouth was still open. "Hey, get a hold of yourself," I nudged him.

"You're right," he whispered. "We're here. I cannot blow this. I cannot blow this. I cannot blow this."

"You know if you keep telling yourself not to blow this," I warned, "then you're gonna blow this."

T-Bone realized I was right and took a couple of deep breaths. I heard giggles around the corner and soon our three friends from Long Branch emerged. They looked so happy and casual and T-Bone looked as stiff as a knight in shining armor.

"Hi, guys," I said and waved.

"Hi, everyone," said Tessy, as John and Lucia waved. "Is anyone hungry?"

We all looked at T-Bone, who seemed unable to blink. I grabbed his hand and raised it for him.

"Why don't we bring out a platter?" Lisa suggested, sensing everyone felt awkward asking for anything.

There was another boy behind Lucia and when we were introduced to him we learned he was Lucia's twin brother, Joey. We were talking with John, Lucia, and Joey while Lisa and Tessy made a platter and grabbed some drinks. When T-Bone saw the platter, I thought he was going to faint again. It was enormous and they told us there was plenty more where that came from. That had to ease T-Bone's mind, I thought.

Usually, we would have waited a little while, but today was different. My dad reached in first and we quickly followed. My parents each grabbed a lobster tail, my brother and sisters selected cookies, and I jumped on a giant éclair. We took our first bites and started oohing and ahhing when I realized T-Bone hadn't taken anything.

"Don't you like dessert?" asked John.

"Sure," T-Bone replied.

"Then pick something," he said, pointing to the tray.

Just when I was about to drag T-Bone to a corner and slap him, the one and only thing that could have snapped him out of his daze happened. Mama walked in. In T-Bone's mind, there must have been a yellow glow around her head. Face to face with his idol, I expected him to just stare at her. Boy, was I wrong.

"Mama!" he yelled as he ran over and hugged her. "Mama! Look, it's Mama!"

I looked at my mom and thought the lemonade was gonna shoot out her nose. Well, that's it, I thought. It should be about five seconds until the doormen come running in to escort us out. All eyes were on T-Bone and it was like watching a runaway train. No one knew his next move.

"Well, you must be Tommy," said Mama as she turned to Lisa. "Boy, you were right. He really is a live wire."

"You're Mama," he shouted. "Do you believe you're Mama? And you have four daughters and one son and you're Mama. There's Maddalena, Mary, Grace, Lisa, and Buddy. And you're Mama. And I have a whisk."

"Wow," she smiled at my parents. "Does this one have an off switch?"

"Unfortunately, no," my dad laughed.

"So, do you need me to stir anything?" he asked, holding up the whisk on a leash. "I know Sal was a great baker and I know he was named Employee of the Century. I'm sure you're real sad that he passed away, so I would help if you need it."

"You're a very sweet boy, aren't you?" she said, grabbing his chin and patting his head. "You're right, Sal was an amazing baker and an amazing friend, just an amazing man altogether. He was part of this family and we all miss him dearly. You're sweet to mention him."

"Thanks," said T-Bone. "I watch every episode with my mom and we love your family; we love everyone. I wish I could have met Buddy Sr., too."

"He would have gotten a kick out of you," said a voice walking in from the back of the kitchen. "That's for sure."

It was Buddy Jr. T-Bone's eyes grew to the size of silver dollars. He came over and shook everyone's hands, even my sisters, and asked us if we needed anything.

"That's Buddy," said T-Bone. "That's Buddy, and that's Mama, and that's Lisa and there's Tessy, John, Lucia, and Joey."

"Don't forget Mary," said a voice coming from around another corner. "You weren't going to forget me, were you?"

"That's Mary," T-Bone repeated as if he was on auto-pilot. "She's Lucia and Joey's mom and Mama is Mary's mom. And Lisa is Tessy, John, and baby Bella's mom."

"Is he thinking out loud?" asked Buddy. "What's the matter with this one?"

"I think he's always like that," Tessy whispered. "He acted like this when we met him in Long Branch."

"So you guys are the Official Junior Ambassadors for New Jersey?" Buddy asked.

"Actually, we're about to be named the Official Junior Ambassadors," I clarified. "So far, we're still unofficial."

"Not getting paid, huh?" he asked.

"No, but even when we become official, we still don't get paid," I said.

"This one over here doing your negotiating?" he joked, pointing at T-Bone. "So, from one guy with a nickname to another, how'd you get the name T-Bone?"

"My name starts with a T?" he asked, as if he wasn't sure.

"Well, I got mine from my father, you know, being I was the only son," he explained.

"And he was the baby of the family," teased Mary.

"It's true," said Lisa. "Our father was named Bartolo and his nickname was Buddy. My brother is also named Bartolo and his nickname is Buddy Jr."

"You know," said T-Bone, waking up from his fog, "a lot of people think your name is Carlo."

"That's true," said Mama. "Since the television show, people think the bakery is named after him or his father. Believe it or not, my husband, Buddy, bought this bakery in 1964 and kept the name out of respect. In over one hundred years, there have only been two owners."

"That's pretty cool," said T-Bone. "How did you meet Buddy Sr.? Were you a customer?"

"It's a beautiful story," Lisa and Mary said together. "Jinx, you owe me a soda."

We laughed when they even said jinx at the same time. Then, Mary started telling the story. We could tell they were sisters because they finished each other's sentences.

"You see, my mom worked here when she was 13 years old," Mary began.

"My father was completely smitten with her and he admired her free spirit," added Lisa. "He came home from the bakery and told his mother that he met the girl he would marry. My grandmother came in the next day to check her out."

"Oh, are you telling Mom and Dad's story?" asked a woman walking down the stairs.

"Yeah, you tell the next part," said Lisa. "Oh, everyone, this is my sister, Grace, and behind her is…"

"Maddalena," said T-Bone, "and your husband is Chef Mauro, a master baker, and Grace, your husband is Joey, and he's not only a baker, but a firefighter."

"Who's the mind-reader?" asked Maddalena. "Are these the boys coming to visit our Tessy?"

"We're the ambassadors for New Jersey," said T-Bone.

"Very nice," said Grace. "We love New Jersey, too. We're really happy that you're sharing our state with everyone."

"So anyway," said Maddalena, "our dad fell in love with our mom immediately, but he was eight years older than her. After my grandmother came in, she told our dad that she was too young. He told her he would wait for her."

"And as soon as she turned seventeen, they were married. My dad told her she would have to learn everything about the bakery, because they would be partners at home and partners in the business. So she learned how to do the bookkeeping and they stayed married until our dad passed away in 1994," said Lisa.

"Wow, that's such an amazing story," my mom said,

145

squeezing Mama's hand. "I have goosebumps."

"Me, too," said Lisa.

"So how many grandkids do you have?" asked my dad.

"Fourteen," said Mama. "And I'm proud to say, just like their parents, they consider this bakery a second home, too."

"It's funny," said Tessy. "So many kids think it's the most amazing place to visit and I'm here all of the time. Sometimes my cousins and I pass out samples to the people in line or sometimes we play games with the customers who are waiting to come in."

"You are so, so, so very lucky," said T-Bone. "Every kid in America would love to do that."

"Great. Here's a tray," said Buddy. "Come back in when you're out of cake."

"Okay," said T-Bone, more than happy to pass out the samples and let everyone wonder who he was.

"No, no, I'm just kidding," said Buddy. "But boy, we could have a lot of fun with this one."

"I say we should hire him," said cousin Frankie, usually the guy getting pranked.

"I could go stand in the alley if you want," said T-Bone,

practically begging Buddy and his crew to dump water and flour on him. "You know, just standing there, not paying attention, just kind of hanging out."

"We've got enough guys doing that," he laughed. "How about a tour and you give us a hand?"

T-Bone immediately shot me a look that said *see, you should've tied some kitchen tools to your belt*. I wondered what kind of work we'd be doing. If my calculations were correct, we should have tied brooms and mops to our belt loops. Luckily, I was wrong.

After a tour of the bakery, the equipment, and Buddy's office, we gathered around a large table. Mama, Buddy, his sisters, and the bakers gave us a mini lesson in baking. Even my sisters were able to get involved without destroying the place. Tessy was giving me and Timmy some pointers and T-Bone planted himself between Mama and Buddy. He was pouring a bag of sugar into a giant mixer, while still holding his nine-inch whisk. The bowl was bigger than my sisters, so I wasn't sure what he thought that little whisk would do. When the ingredients were mixed, I saw him stick the whisk inside the giant bowl. Two seconds later, his arm emerged from the bowl with only the whisk handle.

 Oh, no, I thought. He just lost a whisk in the batter. He looked at me in desperation, terrified to tell Buddy what happened. I knew he wanted his idol to like him and remembered how he saved me during our debate. I motioned for him to switch places and he seemed confused. I started making faces and wildly pointing. When no one was paying attention, we made the switch. As soon as I sat down I confessed to T-Bone's blunder.

"Excuse me, Buddy. I'm really sorry, but I saw a lump and thought I should use the whisk to break it apart. It looks like the whisk broke in the batter," I said, holding up the pitiful little handle.

"You put that little whisk in this big batter?" he asked.

"I'm really sorry, I was just trying to help."

"I get that kind of help all of the time," he laughed.

"Careful, Buddy," said Lisa, "we could tell them some stories about you."

"Oh, don't get me started." Mama shook her head and smiled as the whole Valastro clan burst into laughter.

I had to give it to T-Bone's intuition: this family and bakery were the real deal. They were so close and you could see that even though they probably had their share of disagreements, they had each other's backs. Always a good judge of character, T-Bone sensed it right through the television. I was glad I fooled Buddy into thinking it was me who lost the little whisk in the jumbo batter. It would've crushed T-Bone if he thought Buddy was upset with him.

While the adults were talking, Tessy, John, Joey, and Lucia took us up to their Uncle Buddy's office. They were telling us about some of the celebrities that have come into the bakery. T-Bone's eyes started to glaze over again.

"So, do you feel famous?" I asked as the kids all squished into one big, black leather chair.

"Do you get excited every time you come to the bakery?" asked T-Bone.

They all giggled and told us that they've been coming to the bakery since they were born. They did admit that when they went outside with their mothers and people called their names, they felt a little famous. What they *really* loved was bringing treats outside to the fans waiting in line. I thought that said a lot about the family. With shows and millions of fans, the kids enjoyed passing treats out the most. I decided if I became a philanthropist, I would make sure my kids enjoyed the giving part of it, too.

"Hey, what's going on in here?" Buddy asked as he entered his office. "Some kind of meeting of the minds?"

The cousins started giggling and T-Bone turned a rather interesting shade of red, *again*.

"We're just talking," I said, hoping he wasn't upset.

"Speaking of talking, Nicky," he motioned for me to come into the hall. "I'd like to talk to you in private."

"Sure," I said as I followed him into the hallway and toward the upstairs kitchen. Oh, no, I thought. He must be really upset about the whole whisk thing. I started mentally adding all of the money I had in my four socks at home. Hopefully, it was enough to pay for the batter.

"Listen, Nick," he said, only six inches from my nose, "I know what you did in there."

"You do?" I asked, wondering what else T-Bone did.

"Listen, I was a kid your age once and my wife, Lisa, and I have four kids, so we know about these things."

"I have to be honest," I confessed. "I have no idea what you're talking about."

"A true friend to the end," he said as he patted my head. "That's called being a real stand-up guy."

"Really?" I insisted. "Because I really don't know what you mean."

"You're a rock, kid," he smiled and walked back to his mixer. "You're a real rock."

"My brother's not giving you a hard time, is he?" Lisa laughed as she entered the room.

"No," I said. "I just don't know what he's talking about. He's calling me a stand-up guy and a rock."

"Of course he is," she smiled. "We all admired what you did. Mauro, Joey, and my sisters were just talking about how nice it was."

"How nice what was?" I asked, more confused than ever.

"You really don't know?" she asked.

"I don't have the slightest idea."

Lisa laughed and explained that when the top of the whisk broke off, *everyone knew it was T-Bone's.*

"How did you know?"

"Well, for starters, the look on his face," she laughed. "Of course, there was the fact that it was in the bowl he was working on, and finally, he was the only one who had a whisk tied to his pants."

I turned a little red myself. "I didn't mean to lie. It's just that, as you can see, my friend really feels like he knows your family and he would have been crushed if your brother hollered at him."

"Oh, my brother would have never yelled at him," she explained. "But you didn't know that and you switched places with him. That's pretty impressive."

"Believe it or not, when he's not in front of your family, he's normal," I laughed. "And he always has my back."

"That's how we are," she said. "We're a very big, very close family and I know my dad is so proud of us. Most people don't realize that *the bakery isn't what made us close; our being close is what made the bakery.*"

"That's beautiful," said Mama as she walked by. "What a legacy your father left behind."

I couldn't wait to write my report about the Valastro family and Carlo's Bake Shop. What a great story about a New Jersey family. It had history, it had feeling, and it had hard work. I was surprised no one had turned it into a movie yet. Probably just a matter of time, I thought.

Lisa and my mom gathered all of the kids together and we started saying our goodbyes. Before we left, Mama came to the front door with a t-shirt for everyone and several white boxes tied in string. I could smell the deliciousness through the boxes. After she passed everything out, I realized everyone had a t-shirt except T-Bone. He looked dejected and I wondered why they skipped him. They didn't seem upset about the whisk at all. Just as I was about to raise my hand and tell them, Buddy, Lisa, and the whole gang came in. Tessy and John were holding something in their hands. As they got closer, I could see that it was two t-shirts. Then I noticed what it really was; it was *two signed t-shirts*.

"T-Bone," announced Mama as everyone quieted down. "These two shirts have been signed by everyone in my family just for you. Tessy suggested we give you one to wear and one to save. Fans like you make us proud of the work we do. And make no mistake about it; this is hard work. Don't let the television show fool you. But as hard as it is, meeting people like you is one of the rewards."

"Do you like it? I signed it right here," asked John, pointing to his name.

"I don't know what to say," T-Bone said, far from speechless. "Thank you, Mama. Thank you, Lisa. Thank you, Buddy. Thank you, Maddalena. Thank you, Grace. Thank you, Mary. Thank you, Joey. Thank you, Mauro. Thank you, Tessy, John, Lucia, and Joey."

"You're welcome," they all shouted, before he could start naming their ancestors.

We finished saying our goodbyes and Lisa walked us to the front door. As soon as the crowds saw her, everyone started taking pictures and calling her name. Then they started taking our just-in-case pictures again. T-Bone was wearing one shirt and holding the other shirt in front of him. A man in line noticed it was signed and offered him a hundred dollars for it. T-Bone kept walking with a big smile. As my dad pulled out of the parking garage, T-Bone never said a word. It was the quietest ride we ever had with him in the van.

My mom said we should wait until we get home to untie the boxes and dive into the pastries, but we all knew that would never happen. We polished off a box of cannolis and cookies before we were even off the turnpike. Meeting the Valastro family was so much more interesting than I thought it would be. I really liked the idea of the whole family working together and all of the grandkids growing up together. I wondered if me, Timmy, Maggie, and Emma would grow up that close. Would our kids grow up like they were brother and sister? Would we start a business that we could all do together? *Would T-Bone's kids be there, too?*

Probably, I laughed to myself.

Chapter Ten

Our trip to Hoboken and Carlo's Bake Shop was so memorable that, three days later, T-Bone was still talking about it. I was sure T-Bone would now forget about speaking at the Historic Cold Spring Village. I was wrong.

"Hey, Nick," he said as we walked down the street. "I called Annie last night and told her we could go there this week."

"Oh," I hesitated. "This week isn't good for me."

"Why not?" he asked.

I couldn't think of a good reason that quickly and before I knew it, I was calling my grandfather to see if he could bring us. Not only could he bring us, since we were speaking in the evening, he said we could visit Batsto Village on our way. I wasn't sure what Batsto Village was, so I looked for it on the internet.

"T-Bone, look at this," I said, pointing to the computer screen. "I'm on the Batsto Village website and you aren't going to believe this."

"What is it?"

"It's located in the Wharton State Forest and it was the Batsto Iron Works."

"Did they have a furnace?" he asked. "Did they have a canal? Did they make things for the Revolution? Did they go out of business because the industry changed?"

"Whoa, hold on." I ran my finger across the screen. "It says that Charles Read started the iron works in 1766. There was bog ore which was mined from the banks of the streams and rivers, wood from the forests became the charcoal for fuel, and water became the power for manufacturing. And yes, it says here that they made cooking pots, kettles, and supplies for the Revolution."

"Wow," he exclaimed. "This state is so cool. Did I ever tell you how cool New Jersey is?"

"I think you mentioned it. It looks like there were several owners over the years. They made iron and when that industry declined, they made glass."

"Did people live there?"

"Here, let me read this part from the site," I began. "During the iron-making and glass-making periods at Batsto Village, there were hundreds of people working and living in the village. They needed homes in which to live, so a sawmill was necessary to cut lumber for building homes. The gristmill was built for processing grain. The corn was kept in a nearby corncrib. A storage place for the processed grain was needed. Products that were not naturally available had to be purchased, therefore, a General Store was built. The blacksmith was a necessary part of the community, as was a wheelwright. Different types of barns were erected for the storage of wagons, equipment, and to house animals. The workers planted gardens and orchards. They raised animals for food. A piggery was built for slaughtering the pigs. Without refrigeration, an ice house had to be constructed. Religion was important to the workers, so churches were built nearby. Eventually, a post office helped to speed communication between Batsto and other towns."

"And your grandfather will bring us there?" he asked.

"It was his idea," I laughed.

We spent a couple of days preparing for our speech and our trip to Batsto. Until recently, I had never heard of a blast furnace or an iron ore bog. Suddenly, I knew about the Allaire Village, the Rockaway furnaces, and Batsto Village. Now, if I could learn to speak in front of people.

The morning of our Batsto/Cape May trip arrived quicker than I hoped, mostly because I dreaded giving a speech or debating. T-Bone finally arrived without his Cake Boss shirt and we headed south. My grandfather drove down a series of back roads to get to the village and we were both impressed that he did it without a GPS. When we arrived, we headed to the Visitors Center to get some information and purchase tickets for the mansion. T-Bone pulled out his sock and bought a few postcards and a magnet. Since we had to be in Cape May later, we decided to do the self -guided village tour.

With a map in hand, we headed out. I was picturing kids living in the village while their parents worked and did the things all parents do: taking care of their homes, laundry, cleaning, cooking, etc. We saw the cottages and my grand-father read that the workers lived in single-family dwellings that typically had three rooms downstairs, two rooms upstairs, and an attic. There were also some duplex homes and, during the Wharton era, rent was about two dollars per month.

"Hey, I could even afford that," said T-Bone.

"Now, that's my kind of house," I said, pointing to the mansion. We arrived for our tour and soon learned that it had 32 rooms, 14 of which were open to the public for tours.

"I'm glad to see this one wasn't demolished," T-Bone sighed as we entered the front door.

"It looks like they were expecting us," I observed, pointing to an amazing dining room with the table already set. We continued our tour, admiring some bedrooms, the library, and the parlors.

"I wonder what this cost every month," wondered T-Bone.

"I'd say more than four socks' worth of money," my grandfather winked.

It turned out that there were over 3 dozen restored buildings and the grounds were just as impressive. The Batsto River snaked around the village and there was even a light breeze. At the General Store, workers from the village could purchase everything from fruits and vegetables to guns and farm equipment. As we walked through the village, we checked out the barns, the piggery, the gristmill, the carriage house, and the post office. Not only was the village historic, the post office was, too. It was one of the four oldest post offices currently operating in the United States. It was opened in 1852 by Jesse Richards, one of Batsto's most prominent ironmasters, and served the community for many years. It closed in 1870 when the local economy failed, but reopened in the 1880s. It closed again in 1911, and was reopened by the Batsto Citizens Committee in 1966. As an historic structure, it was never assigned a zip code, so all stamps were hand-canceled.

"I wish I had something to mail," said T-Bone.

"How about the postcards you bought? You could mail one of them to your mom," my grandfather suggested.

"And I could mail the other one to *someone else*, too," he said mysteriously.

"You could do that," my grandfather laughed.

T-Bone grabbed two of the postcards in his bag and quickly wrote his messages. He covered the postcard as if he were protecting the answers on an exam. When he was finished, he went to the counter to mail them.

"All done," he said, putting his change in his pocket.

"Are you boys ready to check out the furnace and the Batsto River?" asked my grandfather.

"Sounds like a plan," I answered.

My grandfather told us the Batsto Lake and the Batsto River were the major reasons for the location of the village and iron furnace. The rivers were a source of bog ore. The lake was created by the dam, which allowed boats to move bog iron from rivers and streams to the iron furnace. The lake also provided water power for the sawmill and grist-mill."

"Do people use it now?" I asked.

"Well, fishing is permitted, as well as canoeing, and the Nature Center has eight canoes available for guided nature trips on the lake."

"Can you swim?" asked T-Bone. "Because I'm pretty sure if I go in a canoe, I'll end up swimming."

We all laughed, trying to imagine T-Bone actually staying in a canoe. Soon, we stumbled upon the furnace. It was hard to believe that a whole village was created because of the furnace. I thought it was a shame that they couldn't make the iron there anymore and then I remembered what my parents told us about progress.

It was getting to be lunchtime and we knew we still had to drive to Historic Cold Spring Village. My grandfather said it would take us a little over an hour and T-Bone reminded him to add time for lunch. My grandfather told us not to worry about lunch, he was bringing us to one of my grandmother's favorite restaurants.

"Down here?" I asked.

"Absolutely," he winked. "Whenever we come to Atlantic City, we always eat at Joe's Maplewood Inn. We've been eating there for years."

"How long have they been there?" asked T-Bone.

"As long as I can remember. They've been around over 60 years. Joe Italiano started the restaurant and now the family owns three," he explained.

"They're like the Valastros," said T-Bone. "Is it on the way?"

"Well, it's a little out of the way, but it'll be worth it."

He wasn't joking. The food was fantastic. T-Bone and I both decided to have the meatball sandwich while my grandfather ordered something I had never heard of: a steakplant parmigiano sandwich. It was a combination of steak and eggplant with provolone cheese. He savored every bite. When our server asked about dessert, we laughed. We could barely move, let alone eat more!

As we headed to the car, I started getting nervous. I would have been happy to head north and forget the whole thing, but I knew T-Bone would never hear of it. Plus, as my dad would have reminded me, we made a commitment. It took about ninety minutes to reach the village and since we were early, we decided to find Annie at the Visitors Center.

"We are all so curious to hear what you have to say," said Annie.

"Me, too," I mumbled to myself.

"Why don't you spend some time in the village and then we can meet at the Grange for dinner before you speak?"

"That sounds great," said T-Bone.

As we walked around, I kept asking him if he wanted to practice. T-Bone kept laughing, saying too much practice would make us sound stale. It's better than awkward silence, I thought. We found ourselves in the print shop as the printer was using a very old machine to print the village logo on paper bags. I thought it was pretty cool

162

that they finished the bags there. We took a wagon ride around the village and stopped by the ice cream shop. It was getting warm and some cold ice cream sounded good.

Around 5:30 we headed to the Grange. My grandfather ordered a seafood pie and I ordered a grilled cheese. When it was T-Bone's turn, he looked at the waiter and said, "I'll take the *Jimmy*." We weren't sure what he had ordered and when it arrived, we were just as confused.

"What is it?" I asked.

"A spaghetti-o taco." He smiled and took a big bite. "And it's delicious."

As much as I enjoyed my dinner, my thoughts kept returning to our speech. I wanted to use pictures on a computer and make it like a movie in a very dark room. T-Bone had decided that we should paint pictures with our words. As the clock kept ticking, I felt like I had forgotten something-- possibly my paintbrush.

We ate with Annie, her husband, Joe, and Clare from the General Store. Everyone was laughing and enjoying their meal while I pretended to be listening. When dinner was over, we headed to the Visitors Center. Every week during their speaker series they had a nice crowd and this was no different. We stood next to Annie at a podium and I considered making a run for it. Before I could take a step, she was introducing us.

"Good evening, everyone," she began. "Tonight we are pleased to have two speakers. While they are considerably younger than our average speaker, they have been doing something that is sorely needed by the state of New Jersey: *they are talking about it*. Not only are they talking about New Jersey, Nicky and Tommy are about to be named New Jersey's Official Junior Ambassadors and they have been providing the state with reports about the dozens of places they have visited so far. And these reports have motivated families to get out there and see New Jersey. They are *introducing New Jersey to New Jersey* and I am pleased to introduce them to you."

While everyone clapped, Annie slipped away from the microphone and T-Bone stepped up.

"Good evening," he said. "My friend, Nicky, and I are not here to tell you that New Jersey is an amazing state; we're here to tell you why it's an amazing state. Please, raise your hands if you are from New Jersey."

Every hand went up and I wasn't sure where he was going with this. He then asked the audience to raise their hands if they thought they knew a lot about their state. Every hand went up. He asked them if they knew about the state's history and once again, every hand went up. I decided if his next question involved their favorite colors, I was leaving.

"For a while now," he continued. "Nicky and I have been finding, visiting, and reporting on great places all around the state. Nicky's grandfather over there and his parents have been lugging us all over so we can remind people of what makes New Jersey special. Not only have we learned so much, we have also realized that there's always more to learn. And that's important. Even if you think you know New Jersey, there's so much more. Nick, why don't you tell them about some of the things we've learned."

Dum, dee, dum, dum, dum played in my head. I looked at T-Bone and looked at the audience. I immediately decided I shouldn't look at the audience. There was a woman in the back smiling, so I decided to look at her.

"T-Bone, I mean, Tommy, is right. There's a lot," I said, and backed away from the podium.

T-Bone looked at me like one of those pageant moms who sits in the audience doing the dance along with their kid. Except I wasn't dancing, I was freezing up and my face was on fire. This is bad, I thought. Annie is going to wish she had never invited us.

"My friend is right," said T-Bone, leaning in toward the podium, not missing a beat. "There's a real lot. Take the Jersey shore with its 128 miles of coastline. This historic village is an amazing place for a family to spend the day. Add the beach and Washington Street mall and you have a two-day trip. Bring an RV and it's an adventure. Or visit Atlantic City with your kids. You don't need to be a gambler to enjoy the world's first and longest boardwalk, the saltwater taffy, or the aquarium and the lighthouse."

165

"Don't forget Ripley's Believe It or Not," I said softly.

"Exactly," T-Bone said with a smile. "And right down the road you can visit Lucy the Elephant, an historic landmark and the only time you can climb to the top of a 65-foot elephant's back."

"Ooh, Salem County," I said, suddenly forgetting about the microphone and the audience, "you can see a world-class rodeo or take a boat ride to the three forts that once protected the Delaware River. They have re-enactors and events, too."

We went on for almost 30 minutes and could have kept going. We discussed New York teams playing in New Jersey and reminded people that it started long before the Giants and Jets. That first baseball game in Hoboken was actually played by *two New York teams*. Then T-Bone told them about Patriot's Week in Trenton.

"The city of Trenton is more than the state capital, it's where our country's fortune turned around. Had General Washington lost in Trenton, we may have lost the war. During Patriot's Week, you can see two battle re-enactments, attend a ball with colonial re-enactors, take tours of the city and its historic spots, or visit two of our favorite places, the Old Barracks and the Trent House."

"Talk about stepping back in time," I interrupted. "These two locations are amazing and we are hoping that Trenton uses them as the foundation of an historic revitalization.

At least, that's what my grandfather said should happen and we agree with him."

My grandfather proudly smiled and winked at me. Suddenly, a hand went up and the smiling woman told everyone that she and her husband attend Patriot's Week every year and she's so happy we are encouraging families to attend. "It's not just for history buffs like myself," she smiled. "It's fun and something all New Jersey families should enjoy."

In the front row, a young boy raised his hand and T-Bone called on him.

"My name is Jimmy Papperman and I think your next adventure should be at the Lucky Charm Horse Farm in Dennisville."

"Tell me more," said T-Bone, resting his chin on his fists. "Go on, Jimmy."

"First you start your tour by meeting my miniature horse, Cinnamon Sugar Pop Tart. I call him Pop Tart for short. You could help tack Pop Tart up for a horse and buggy ride with me as your driver. As you climb aboard the buggy and travel down Lucky Charm Way, you will meet our fun-loving goats, stopping for a game of tag."

"No way," said T-Bone, "you have all of these animals *and a horse and buggy?*"

"That's not all," Jimmy continued, "the second stop would be at the pigs. Their names are Wilbur, Hogzilla, and Tight End. As you climb aboard the buggy to continue the ride, you'll see the dogs, also known as the licking committee. The next stop is the chicken coop where you can meet my prized-winning chicken, Chickadee, and collect eggs in a basket. You may even be lucky enough to find a blue or brown egg. Now, after the chickens, you will meet two famous American Quarter Horses named Zippy Dippin' and Kizzy's Hot Rod. You can feed them carrots and apples, then it's off to the bunnies. When we're done with the tour we have our own snacks."

"Your chicken has won prizes?" asked T-Bone. "Does it dance?"

"No," Jimmy laughed. "It won in 4-H contests. The club that I'm in is called the Pitchforks & Buckets and it's the oldest livestock club in Cape May County."

"Wow," I said, "that's very cool. We just learned about 4-H and we may even join."

"I'll leave my address and maybe you can stop by one day," he said as he placed a piece of paper on the podium.

"I'll tell you what," said T-Bone. "Maybe you can show us your farm and we can show you Patriot's Week."

"It's a deal," he smiled.

The rest of the evening went much better than I imagined, and since I imagined total doom, that wasn't difficult. When we wrapped up, fifteen minutes longer than scheduled and still with a room full of raised hands, we knew we did a good job. Annie was very pleased. When she went back to the podium, she invited everyone for refreshments with the *Great Allies of History*. T-Bone had a smile from one ear to the other. During the refreshments, people were asking us questions and one teacher told us she uses our reports to teach about New Jersey.

"I want to thank you boys and your grandfather for making the trip down to Cape May. It's so refreshing to see our youngest generation learning about New Jersey and appreciating history," Annie smiled.

"Thanks for having us," I said, shaking her hand.

As we drove home, I felt an enormous sense of relief. Maybe I wasn't as scared to speak in public if it was like a conversation. Maybe it was just the idea of giving a speech and doing all of the talking. As long as T-Bone was there to get things rolling, it wasn't so bad. Maybe one day, I thought, I could do it on my own. For now, though, I was perfectly content playing second fiddle.

Chapter Eleven

The next morning, I decided to start writing the report for Batsto Village. When I was halfway through, the phone rang. It was Billy. He said he had received a letter from a little girl and wanted to send it to us. I told him if I could get a ride, we'd be there later, and he decided to hold off on mailing it. I wondered what it could be.

When T-Bone arrived, we finished our report and discussed our visit to Historic Cold Spring Village. He really enjoyed talking to people about New Jersey and I was secretly glad that he made me go along.

"Good morning, Tommy," my mom said as she poked her head in my room. "I heard you were fantastic last night."

"Thanks, Mrs. A.," he nodded, still grinning.

"Mom, is there any chance you could take us to Trenton to drop off a report to Billy?" I asked.

"Well, that must have been some trip if you've already done your report," she smiled. "I can take you in about an hour."

"Thanks, Mom," I said as she headed down the hall. "Hey, T-Bone, Billy called and he has a letter for us from a girl. He didn't say what it was about, though."

"Do you think she wrote to tell us that we're the Official Junior Ambassadors?" he asked.

"Why would a girl we don't know tell us? Don't you think Billy would call?"

"Actually, every time the phone rings, I expect it to be a reporter," he said. "I've had remarks prepared for weeks."

I shook my head and laughed, but knowing T-Bone's luck, a camera crew would probably show up on his doorstep.

"I was thinking," he said, "there should be a *Hall of Fame* in New Jersey. My dad told me about some of the famous people who were born here and there's a ton of them."

"They should," I answered, not really paying attention.

"I'm serious," he continued. "New Jersey is so important, but that's only because of the people who live here."

"How do you know we don't already have one?" I asked.

"Because I never heard of it," he replied.

I immediately went to the computer and searched for New Jersey Hall of Fame. We were both shocked to see that there was one. We immediately came upon a website that read *The New Jersey Hall of Fame, Celebrating the Garden State.*

"Cool," said T-Bone. "I think I'd like to be in it one day."

"Very well, sir," I said in a grown-up voice. "I'll get them on the phone and tell them to induct you. Hold on, let's see who was in this year's class: Leon Hess, Martha Stewart, John Travolta, Tony Bennett, Queen Latifah, John Basilone, John Bucky Pizzarelli, Bruce Willis, Franco Harris, Joe Theismann, Governor Brendan Byrne, Admiral Halsey and Mary Higgins Clark. I'm sure you were just overlooked. Your nvitation probably got lost in the mail."

"Seriously," he said. "I'm not talking about now, but one day. And I have suggestions of other people they could include, like Annie and Joe Salvatore and the Valastros."

"I agree," I said, "they should be in it. But why would they induct you?"

"Because I plan on doing great things for this state."

"I'd vote for you," said Timmy.

"Really?" T-Bone asked, a little shocked.

"Sure, why not?" he laughed. "Then, if there's a party we can meet the really important people."

172

"Very funny," said T-Bone. "Where are they located? Can we visit?"

As I continued to read, I was impressed. Their mission was to provide examples for children to strive for excellence in whatever endeavor they chose. There would be three regional museums, one in north Jersey, one in Trenton for central Jersey, and one in South Jersey. I liked the fact that it would be easy for anyone in our state to visit. The Trenton Museum was scheduled to open first and I thought about my grandfather's vision for the city. This would be really good for Trenton. They also had traveling exhibits and materials for teachers on their website. When I read everything to T-Bone, his eyes lit up. Instead of being discouraged, he decided that one day he would be inducted as a *Great Ally of History*. If that happened, he'd probably have me up on stage with him. Hopefully, I wouldn't have to give a speech.

"You guys ready?" my mom hollered upstairs.

"Coming," I said as I grabbed my report and memory stick with pictures.

When we arrived at the State House, Billy was already in the hall speaking to another man. When he finished his conversation he came up and thanked us for coming so quickly.

"We went to Batsto Village with my grandfather," I announced as I handed him the envelope.

173

"I have to tell you," he smiled, "since you boys began this project, I have learned so much about our state. We're very lucky to have you both working for New Jersey."

"Does that mean we're official?" asked T-Bone, hoping Billy was ready to make an announcement.

"Not yet," he winked. "But I'm sure it won't be long."

"Do you think we're good enough to get into the New Jersey Hall of Fame?" T-Bone followed up.

"I'd vote for you," he smiled.

"Do you get to vote?" said T-Bone.

"No, but I wouldn't be surprised to read that you boys have been inducted to the Hall of Fame one day."

"Do you have that letter for us?" I quickly changed the subject.

"Oh, yes," he said, pulling it out of a binder and handing it to us. "You may want to put something about this on the website, especially since it's coming from another kid. I have to run now."

We said goodbye and I started reading the letter aloud.

"My name is Lexie Pandullo and I have a very special 6-year-old little brother. My brother, Anthony, was

174

diagnosed with autism when he was just 2 years old. He is the funniest person I know. He really means a lot to me and I would do anything to help him. Every fall Autism Speaks holds their annual walk in Nomahegan Park in Cranford, NJ. My family started the "Property of Pandullo" team to walk for a cure for my little brother. We joined the 7,500 people for the 6th annual North/Central Jersey Walk Now for Autism that was held on Sunday, October 26, 2010.

It was a day filled with excitement. I wore everything blue I could find, including our team shirt. Blue is the official color of autism. There was a lot of food and all sorts of autism awareness stuff like magnets, bracelets, and necklaces. I was so proud to be with my entire family and to meet so many other people walking for the same reason as me. I want to be the big voice that my brother doesn't have. When I walked with my aunt around the pond and through the woods, there were so many people with all different team shirts. I'm so glad I walked to help all kids with autism. I can't wait to do it again this October!"

"Wow," said my mom, wiping a tear from her eye. "What a wonderful big sister."

"Lexie should be in the Hall of Fame," said T-Bone. "She's trying to cure her brother's disease. That's huge."

"I know," I agreed. "How can we help her? Mom, do you have any ideas?"

"Well," she sniffled, "you could put that on your website

175

so everyone is aware. Maybe you'll get some people to walk, and if they can't walk, at least to donate. There are so many children who have autism and kids like Lexie can really make a difference."

"Maybe we can walk, too," I suggested.

"That's a wonderful idea," my mom agreed, giving me one of her combination hug/hair tosses. Since we became unofficial ambassadors, we learned about Ryan, little Joey, and now Anthony. It always reminded me of how lucky I was and how everyone who was lucky should be helping. My mom was right; kids could make a difference, and I was going to write a report about Lexie and Anthony. Maybe T-Bone was right and she would end up in the Hall of Fame for helping to cure this disease.

When we left the State House, my mom didn't head straight home. She told us she had to make one stop. Oh, no, I thought, we're going shopping. I was hoping it wasn't for furniture or food. I dreaded those shopping trips. We turned into a shopping center called The Shoppes at Hamilton.

"Hey, they spelled *shops* wrong," said T-Bone. "And no one told them."

"They didn't spell it wrong," I laughed. "That's the fancy way to spell it."

"Oh," he said, shaking his head.

"Where are we going?" I asked.

"Well, I have to pick up a few things for your sisters at the Learning Express," she said.

"You mean we're going to a toy store?" I asked in disbelief. Usually my mom ordered most of the toys for my sisters from catalogs. It must have been the teacher in her, but she loved educational toys.

"Just for a minute. I always order from the catalog and didn't know they had several stores in New Jersey."

The store was really cool and I recognized most of the items from their catalogs. Every time one came, Maggie would get a marker and circle everything in it. It was probably good that Maggie wasn't there. My mom grabbed a counting cookies game and a string the alphabet game while T-Bone tried every toy that wasn't nailed down. While my mom paid, T-Bone was gliding through the store on a plasma car.

"Anyone hungry?" asked my mom.

It was noon, so she really should have known the answer. We headed to a nearby restaurant called Wildflowers Too. There was a big bar in the middle and tables on both ends. A woman named Amanda asked us where we preferred to sit and T-Bone told her he would enjoy sitting by the fireplace. My mom told her the enclosed patio would be just fine and she led us in that direction.

Amanda brought us some water and asked if we would like anything else to drink. We placed our drink order and looked over the menu. This was another one of those situations where there were too many things I liked on the menu. I changed my mind several times and decided on a grilled cheese. There was a girl sitting with her dad and brothers at the next table. T-Bone glanced over and once again introduced himself.

"Hi, I'm T-Bone and this is our first time here," he began. "I was wondering what you ordered."

"Hi, I'm Jessica and these are my brothers, Patrick and Timothy," she said. "We always order the same things."

"So you're regulars?" he asked.

"Definitely," said Patrick. "My sister always gets the mozzarella sticks; she ranks them number one of all the places we go. Then she orders a grilled cheese and so does my little brother."

"Hi, I'm Timmy," he said. "My best friend is Wyatt and his brother is Dalton and I'm a fast runner."

"Wow!" said T-Bone. "Hi, Timmy. My friend Nicky over there has a brother named Timmy, too. How old are you?"

"Boron," the little boy answered, holding up five fingers.

"Excuse me?" said T-Bone.

"Oh, he memorized the periodic table of elements," said Jessica. "Boron is number five."

"I don't even know what that means," T-Bone laughed. "So what do you like to order, Mr. Boron?"

"Food," he giggled. "And my name is not Mr. Boron, it's Tim-o-thy and my best friend is Wyatt and his brother is Dalton, and I run fast, don't you remember?"

"I will now," T-Bone laughed.

"I always get the soup and the chicken tenders," said Patrick. "They're fantastic."

"You've really never been here before?" asked Jessica.

"No, we don't live around here," T-Bone explained. "We were just visiting the toy store."

"The new one at The Shoppes?" asked Jessica. "My mom buys toys there because they're educational. It's a good thing they're really, really fun, too. We love that store."

"My friend's mom brought us there," said T-Bone pointing. "She's a teacher, so she's all about that educational stuff."

"So is our mom," Jessica laughed and returned to her meal.

"So, have we decided?" Amanda asked as she returned to the table and placed our drinks down.

"I'll have your number-one-ranked mozzarella sticks and a grilled cheese with fries," said T-Bone.

"I see you've met Jessica," she laughed.

"Well, I'll take the soup and chicken tenders with fries," I said, changing my original order.

"And I suppose you've met Patrick?"

"Sure did," I said, giving him a thank-you wave.

I had to hand it to the kids at the next table; they were spot on with their recommendations. My mom freelanced and ordered a big salad. She said it was fantastic. T-Bone and I practically licked our plates clean.

"So, how was it?" asked Amanda.

"Superb," said T-Bone, pulling out a new word.

"Wow, superb is a pretty big compliment," she smiled. "I'll tell my dad."

"Is he the cook?" I asked.

"No," she smiled, "we're partners."

"You mean you're the owner?" asked T-Bone. "And you took our order *and* brought our food?"

"Sure," she said. "One of the servers wasn't feeling well, so I told her to stay home and I came in for her."

"But you're an *owner*," said T-Bone. "You're the boss."

"I'm an owner in a family business," she laughed. "And when it's your business, no job is too small."

"I'm thinking about starting a family business," T-Bone said, "but I'm probably gonna use *his* family."

"Just be prepared to work hard," she warned.

When we got in the car, T-Bone was even more excited about family businesses. He was trying to figure out how he could have a family business with my family, promote New Jersey, be a philanthropist, and wind up in the Hall of Fame while writing a play called *New Jersey*. I wasn't even sure if that was possible, but if it was, I knew he would be the guy to do it. And knowing T-Bone, he had probably already written his acceptance speech.

When we got home, I wrote a report about Lexie's brother, using her letter, exactly as she had given it to us. I hoped her determination would cause families to participate in the walk or donate to help find a cure. I knew if Timmy, Maggie, or Emma had autism, I'd try to do the same thing. It seemed so unfair that so many families had to watch little kids suffer. There should be a law, I thought, that every kid should have a great childhood without diseases or poverty or family troubles. When you're an adult, you have to make your own way. But when you're a kid, you should only worry about which cartoon to watch or which flavor ice cream you should choose. I figured those of us who were lucky sometimes got so wrapped up in our own lives that we forgot how lucky we really were. T-Bone had the right idea. Dream big and make things happen by working hard. Every family business we came across said it was really hard work and yet they all seemed so happy. Maybe working hard was the key to success. Maybe overcoming adversity didn't happen because a person was strong; maybe overcoming adversity is what made a person strong.

That night, before I went to bed, I played tea party with my sisters. They were shocked when I suggested it, especially because I always gave them an excuse. I had given them so many excuses that when I offered to play, Maggie said, "Is it later now?" When I finished the tea party, I stopped by Timmy's room and asked him if he wanted to play 500 Rummy. He was so excited. He didn't even ask why I wanted to play with him. It took two hours until he won, partly because I kept throwing away my good cards. When the game was over, I felt good. It wasn't a family business, but I figured family fun was the way to start.

The places we had visited recently and the people we had met made a huge impression on me. I hoped they would make an impression on the kids who visited our website. Maybe they would slow down and take some time to enjoy what they had and more importantly, who they had in their lives. It was a start, I thought.

Chapter Twelve

A week had gone by and T-Bone and I had lined up several odd jobs. We even added a fifth sock to our former four sock operation; the fifth sock was for autism. Our customers were always complimenting us on what hard workers we were and how respectful we treated them. It felt good to not only get paid to do a job, but to know we did our best. I was just finishing up some weeding for Mrs. Conner when I realized it must have been dinnertime. I raced home on my bike and arrived just as my mom was taking a meatloaf out of the oven.

My dad walked in right behind me and said he ran into some of our customers at his store. They told him what fine boys T-Bone and I were. My dad was really proud. He then told me not to schedule any jobs for the next day.

"Why?" I asked. "What's up?"

"We're going to the Liberty Science Center," he said.

"That place is so cool. Can T-Bone come?"

"Of course he can," my mom answered before my dad had a chance to moan.

"School will be starting soon and I thought we should get in one more day trip," he explained. "I know you like to visit new places and we've already been there, but I think it'll be fun."

"That's great, Dad," I agreed, "because last time we went we were just kids, we weren't ambassadors."

"Exactly," he smiled.

"Should I print the directions and schedule?" I asked.

"Just see what time they open," he said. "I remember exactly how to get there."

After dinner, I checked their website and saw that they opened at 9:00 a.m. We decided to get an early start and told T-Bone to be at our house by 7:00 a.m. Of course, our doorbell rang at 6:00 a.m. We headed toward the turnpike with a notebook, a Flip Cam, and batteries. My mom checked with my dad to see if he remembered how to get there and he laughed. He told her he only needed to go somewhere once to know how to get there. "I keep it all up here," he said, pointing to his head.

Traffic was heavy and it seemed like everyone in the world must have been on the turnpike that morning. The last time we went, we were in the limo T-Bone had won for the day, so I really had no idea how to get there. For some reason, my dad got off at Exit 10. Before we knew it, we were on something called the Outer Bridge.

"Honey, is this right?" asked my mom.

"Yeah, it's a shortcut," he said, sounding a little agitated.

"This definitely doesn't look right, Mr. A.," T-Bone observed. "You might want to recalculate."

"Hey, look, it says Welcome to New York," I announced as I read the sign. "I don't think this is right."

"It's fine," said my dad, clearly trying to figure out where we were while navigating through the morning rush hour.

"Hon, we're in Staten Island," my mom whispered.

"I know," he said, trying to remain calm. "I know."

"Maybe we should stop and ask someone for directions," T-Bone suggested.

"We don't need directions," my dad insisted. "I know right where we are."

"So do I," said T-Bone. "We're in Staten Island."

My dad had this thing about directions. He claimed he could never get lost and that he remembered every place he had ever been. Even if he got lost, he played it off as if he meant to go that way.

After driving for some time, we arrived at the Staten Island

Ferry. My sisters had to go to the bathroom, so my mom brought them into the terminal. My dad looked so confused.

"Hey," my mom said as she returned to the van. "I was talking to a woman inside and she asked the girls if we were going on the ferry. When I told her we were lost, I mean on our way to the Liberty Science Center, she suggested we take the kids on a ferry ride, first."

"Why would we park here and take a ferry?" my dad asked slowly and quietly, like a volcano before the eruption.

"Because it's not just for commuters, it's also a tourist attraction and gives riders great views of the city and the Statue of Liberty," she said.

"Can we go, Dad?" asked Timmy. "I really want to go on a ferry."

"We're on our way to the science center," my dad explained. "Plus, do you have any idea how much it would cost for seven people to ride a ferry round trip?"

"I do," my mom smiled. "It's free."

"What?" my dad asked, looking even more confused.

"It's free and it's a 30-minute ride to Manhattan and a 30-minute ride back," she explained. "We're already here and it would be a great way to see New Jersey from the water."

"Well, since it's on the way and it's free, I guess we can do it," he said, still sticking with his this-was-all-part-of-my-plan theory.

"Perfect," my mom smiled as she grabbed the diaper bag. "The next one leaves in a few minutes."

I had to hand it to my dad; his mistake was fantastic. The ferry ride was unbelievable. The views of New York City, the Statue of Liberty, and New Jersey were breathtaking. It was definitely one of those pleasant surprises. We ended up sitting next to Liz, the same woman my mom had met earlier. When she found out we had never been to Staten Island, she laughed. "I'm not surprised, Staten Island gets very little respect."

"Hey, we're from Jersey," I said. "We know all about the no-respect thing."

"The funny thing is that, just like over in Jersey, Staten Island is a beautiful place with amazing parks, open spaces, history, and family entertainment," she explained.

"Did you say history?" asked T-Bone.

"Absolutely," she smiled. "There's the Conference House, named in honor and commemoration of the famous peace conference of 1776, when Continental Congress representatives John Adams, Edward Rutledge, and Benjamin Franklin met with the King's representative, Lord Richard Howe, at Colonel Christopher Billopp's home on Staten Island. The British would not agree to any terms that included independence and the colonists were only authorized to settle if independence was part of the deal. So, their efforts to stop the war failed and the rest is history."

"You sure know a lot about history," said T-Bone. "And Staten Island."

"I should," she smiled. "I teach at the Staten Island Academy."

"Oh, that explains it," I said. "My mom is a teacher, too."

"We're *New Jersey's Unofficial-Soon-to-be-Official Junior Ambassadors,*" said T-Bone, as he explained our duties.

"That's pretty impressive," she said. "Maybe you could tell New Jersey about Staten Island, too, since we have so much in common."

"I don't know," said T-Bone, pointing to me. "Every time I suggest visiting Hawaii or some other place, this one over here tells me it has to be in New Jersey."

"I understand," she said. "But if you look at a map, you'll see just how close we are to you. Plus, so many Staten Islanders visit New Jersey; maybe New Jersey can pay us a visit sometime. We'd love to have you."

"She has a point," said T-Bone. "What else do you have besides the awesome ferry and the Conference House?"

"We have the Staten Island Zoo, Fort Wadsworth under the Verrazano Narrows Bridge, Historic Richmondtown, Great Kills Park and Beach, the Staten Island Yankees, the Snug Harbor Cultural Center, and South Beach," she said. "And there's so many other things, too."

"And you really get no respect?" asked T-Bone. "Because New Jersey is the most misunderstood state around."

"Then we are your sister city," she laughed.

We decided to tell New Jersey about our neighbor who also lives in the shadows of the rest of New York City. My dad said we could spend a little more time checking out Staten Island when the ferry returned. We drove along the coast and found the beaches she had mentioned and even stopped quickly by the Conference House.

"I don't get it," said T-Bone. "What's not to love?"

"I guess it's like being a really good singer, when your brother is a major rock star," I said, trying to come up with an analogy that worked.

We eventually made it to the Bayonne Bridge which connected Staten Island with Bayonne, New Jersey. When I looked at the road atlas, I realized that I always thought Staten Island was part of New Jersey. I never knew it was one of New York City's five boroughs, along with Brooklyn, Bronx, Queens, and of course, Manhattan. Everyone we met had been so friendly and I knew we would be back. My mom suggested we go online and check the events calendar because her new friend, Liz, told her there were great events throughout the year.

We made our way through Bayonne and into Jersey City. Luckily, there were signs telling us which way to go. We finally arrived at the Liberty Science Center. It was already after lunchtime and we didn't trust my dad to find a restaurant, so we ate at the Café Skylines right inside. There were exhibits on skyscrapers, infections, the food chain, and the Hudson River, and we were trying to decide if we were seeing a show at the IMAX Theater. My mom was worried it would scare the girls, but my dad disagreed and bought tickets for a show called "Born to Be Wild." He said they'd love the animals and he was right.

This place had changed since our last visit, so I felt like it was our first time all over again. I wanted to thank the person who invented the Liberty Science Center. I also wanted to thank the guy who posted the turnpike signs everywhere. What a lifesaver.

"So, did everyone have a good day?" asked my mom.

"Awesome," I said. "I can't wait to write both reports."

"*Both reports*?" asked my dad.

"Sure," I explained. "Staten Island will get its own report. I think it's the right thing to do. Then Liberty Science Center will get its own report, too."

When we returned home, my dad ordered a couple of pizzas and my mom made a big salad. While we waited for the pizza to arrive, T-Bone and I started writing about the day. The pictures from the Staten Island Ferry were amazing and we were hoping Billy would use them. After dinner, T-Bone went home and I called my grandfather to tell him about our day.

"That's wonderful," he said when I told him about our adventure. "So many New Jerseyans spend time in Staten Island and vice versa that I think he'll really enjoy it."

"I hope so," I said.

The next morning, I called Billy. When I told him about our two reports, he agreed with my grandfather and welcomed the information and the pictures. With school starting soon, he suggested we mail the reports and pictures so we could get ready. It was hard to believe that the summer was almost over until I thought about all of the places we had visited.

We had covered New Jersey from top to bottom and from end to end, including most of the shore towns. It was cool to think that other people were following in our footsteps. I knew once we became Official Junior Ambassadors we could reach even more people. As I was daydreaming about becoming official, my mom knocked on my door.

"You've got mail," she said in a funny computer voice.

"Really?" I asked. "Is it from the state?"

"No, honey," she shrugged, "but it's really funny."

"Funny?" I asked, as my mom handed me a postcard.

"What's this?"

It was a postcard from Batsto Village. When I turned it over, I realized it was from T-Bone with the following message:

Dear T-Bone, you're doing a good job as an ambassador and they'll make you official sooner or later. Hang in there. Your Friend, T-Bone.

"I don't get it," said my mom. "Why did he send himself a postcard and why did he send it here?"

I looked at the card and laughed. I didn't know what was funnier: that he sent himself a pep-talk postcard or that he was now getting his mail at my house. In the end, I decided the funniest thing was that he signed it *Your Friend*, when clearly...*that was my job*.

The End

Nicky Fifth's New Jersey
Contest Winners

Grand Prize - Tessy Colegrove
Central School, East Hanover, NJ
Carlo's Bake Shop, Hoboken, NJ
● ● ● ● ● ● ● ● ● ● ● ● ● ● ● ● ● ●
2nd Prize (*tie*) - Brooke Bryant
Dr. William Mennies School, Vineland, NJ
Grounds For Sculpture, Hamilton, NJ
2nd Prize (*tie*) -Robert Moran
Mansfield Township ES, Columbus, NJ
Howell Living History Farm, Titusville, NJ
● ● ● ● ● ● ● ● ● ● ● ● ● ● ● ● ● ●

3rd Prize - Melanie Gianino
Packanack ES, Wayne, NJ
Allaire State Park, Wall Township
● ● ● ● ● ● ● ● ● ● ● ● ● ● ● ● ●
Special Guests
Jimmy Papperman
Dennis Township ES, Dennis Township, NJ
Lucky Charm Horse Farm

Lexie Pandullo
Central School, East Hanover, NJ
North/Central Jersey Walk For Autism Speaks

Are You A New Jersey Character?

Submit your favorite New Jersey destination to Nicky Fifth and T-Bone and you could become a character in an upcoming Nicky Fifth book. Write a 3-4 paragraph persuasive essay, selling your idea to Nicky and T-Bone. Make sure your idea is located in New Jersey and hasn't been included in a previous book in the series. Check the website for a list of places already included.

Entries are judged on creativity, writing style, history, and level of persuasion. Do not list numerous locations; focus on one and make sure it is located in New Jersey. To enter, visit www.nickyfifth.com and be sure you have your parents' permission.

Prizes:

1st Prize - $200.00 Barnes & Noble Gift Card
Digital Video Camera
YOUR idea is used in an upcoming book
YOU become a character in the book

2nd Prize - $100.00 Barnes & Noble Gift Card

3rd Prize - $75.00 Barnes & Noble Gift Card

About the Charity

"Property of Pandullo" Team
North/Central Jersey
Walk Now for Autism Speaks

Thanks to Lexie Pandullo for sharing her personal connection with Autism and the work of Autism Speaks. Lexie hopes to find a cure for her younger brother, Anthony, and walks to raise money for Autism Speaks.

Visit www.autismspeaks.org to learn about autism and how you can help. The following facts are from their website and illustrate why everyone's help is needed:

It is estimated that one in every 110 children is diagnosed with autism, making it more common than childhood cancer, juvenile diabetes and pediatric AIDS combined.

An estimated 1.5 million individuals in the U.S. and tens of millions worldwide are affected by autism.

Autism Speaks was founded in 2005 by Bob and Suzanne Wright, grandparents of a child with autism. Their longtime friend, Bernie Marcus donated $25 million to help financially launch the organization.

Since then, Autism Speaks has grown into the nation's largest autism science and advocacy organization, dedicated to funding research into the causes, prevention, treatments and a cure for autism; increasing awareness of autism spectrum disorders; and advocating for the needs of individuals with autism and their families.

About the Author

Lisa Funari Willever wanted to be an author since she was in the third grade. She has been a wedding dress seller, a file clerk, a sock counter (*really*), a hostess, waitress, teacher, and author. While she loved teaching in Trenton, New Jersey, becoming an author has been one of the most exciting adventures of her life. She is a full-time mom and a night-time author who travels all over the world visiting schools. She has been to hundreds of schools in dozens of states, including California, South Dakota, Iowa, South Carolina, Florida, Delaware, Connecticut, New York, Pennsylvania, Ohio, Nevada, Idaho, Utah, Alabama, Louisiana, and even the U.S. Navy base in Sasebo, Japan.

She has written eighteen books for children and new teachers. *A Glove of Their Own* won the 2009 Benjamin Franklin Award. The critically-acclaimed *Chumpkin* was selected as a favorite by First Lady Laura Bush and displayed at the White House; *Everybody Moos at Cows* was featured on the Rosie O'Donnell Show; and *Garden State Adventure* and *32 Dandelion Court* have been selections for the prestigious New Jersey Battle of the Books list.

Lisa, a graduate of Trenton State College, is married to Todd Willever, a captain in the Trenton Fire Department. They reside in Mansfield, New Jersey with their three children, Jessica, Patrick, and Timothy. If you would like to invite Lisa to speak at your school, visit www.franklinmasonpress.com for more details.

Passport to the Garden State

Above each box is the location,
below each box is the actual *Stamp Stop*.

Hamilton Twp. Mercer County	Hamilton Twp. Mercer County	Hamilton Twp. Mercer County
Grounds For Sculpture	Grounds For Sculpture - Rats	Kuser Mansion
Hamilton Twp. Mercer County	Hamilton Twp. Mercer County	Hamilton Twp. Mercer County
Chick and Nello's Homestead Inn	Hamilton Twp. Public Library	Learning Express Toy Store

Passport to the Garden State

Above each box is the location,
below each box is the actual *Stamp Stop*.

Yardville Mercer County	Allentown	Lambertville
Wildflowers Too Restaurant	Horse Park of New Jersey	Howell Living History Farm
Lambertville	Lambertville	Farmingdale
Lambertville Station	Rick's Italian Restaurant	Allaire Village Bakery

Passport to the Garden State

Above each box is the location,

below each box is the actual *Stamp Stop*.

Farmingdale	Swedesboro	Hancock's Bridge Salem County
Allaire Village General Store	Sweetsboro Pastry Shop	Hancock House
Pilesgrove	Pier Village Long Branch	Rockaway
Cowtown Rodeo	Carter & Cavero Old World Oils	Hibernia Diner

Passport to the Garden State

Above each box is the location,

below each box is the actual *Stamp Stop*.

Trenton	Hoboken	Hoboken
Papa's Tomato Pies	Tutta Pasta Restaurant	Carlo's City Hall Bake Shop
Hammonton	Hammonton	Jersey City
Batsto Village	Joe's Maplewood Restaurant	Liberty Science Center